SELECTED WORKS OF PEARL
JEPHCOTT: SOCIAL ISSUES
AND SOCIAL RESEARCH

Volume 4

TIME OF ONE'S OWN

TIME OF ONE'S OWN

Leisure and Young People

PEARL JEPHCOTT

LONDON AND NEW YORK

First published in 1967 by Oliver & Boyd

This edition first published in 2023
by Routledge
4 Park Square, Milton Park, Abingdon, Oxon OX14 4RN

and by Routledge
605 Third Avenue, New York, NY 10158

Routledge is an imprint of the Taylor & Francis Group, an informa business

© 1967 Pearl Jephcott
© 2023 Josephine Koch

All rights reserved. No part of this book may be reprinted or reproduced or utilised in any form or by any electronic, mechanical, or other means, now known or hereafter invented, including photocopying and recording, or in any information storage or retrieval system, without permission in writing from the publishers.

Trademark notice: Product or corporate names may be trademarks or registered trademarks, and are used only for identification and explanation without intent to infringe.

British Library Cataloguing in Publication Data
A catalogue record for this book is available from the British Library

ISBN: 978-1-032-33020-4 (Set)
ISBN: 978-1-032-33373-1 (Volume 4) (hbk)
ISBN: 978-1-032-33387-8 (Volume 4) (pbk)
ISBN: 978-1-003-31944-3 (Volume 4) (ebk)

DOI: 10.4324/9781003319443

Publisher's Note
The publisher has gone to great lengths to ensure the quality of this reprint but points out that some imperfections in the original copies may be apparent.

Disclaimer
The publisher has made every effort to trace copyright holders and would welcome correspondence from those they have been unable to trace.

PLATE I

Some of the 431,000 boys and girls
aged 15-19

Frontispiece

New Foreword to the Reissue of *Time of One's Own*

After graduating from Aberystwyth University in 1921, Pearl Jephcott (1900–1980) spent the next twenty years or so working in what would now be called youth work for youth advice, youth counselling or childhood services. In particular, she focused on the clubs that young people attended and wrote about young people's experiences of growing up and how to organise clubs for girls. She worked in youth clubs across the UK. For example, she gained knowledge of the harsh everyday realities young people experienced in places such as the northeast of England with its heavy industry and traditional working-class culture. In this context, books such as *Clubs for Girls* (1943) advise young women on the ways to behave, what to learn and how to avoid the pitfalls of adult life. Overall, given her experiences, Pearl became sensitised from very early on to challenges facing young people in their work, home, and in their leisure time. To that end, Pearl Jephcott returned to Aberystwyth University and completed an MA degree in 1949 entitled *'Studies of employed adolescent girls in relation to their development and social background'*.

However, it's important to note that when Pearl was writing these early works, 'youth' as a category did not exist as part of the life cycle or as a life stage. You were either a child or an adult with young people exhibiting adult behaviours, preferences, and attitudes as soon as they had left full-time education. For example, children were expected to behave like adults as soon as they entered the world of work. It was only in the 1950s and 1960s that the liminal space of youth began to emerge as a liminal period, childhood, and adulthood, where young people may behave distinctly to either children or adults. Given Pearl Jephcott's concern for how young people spent their leisure time, it is also perhaps no surprise that she returned the problems of youth to this question specifically in her book *A Time of One's Own*.

At its heart, this book is undergirded by a straightforward question – how do young Scots spend their leisure time nowadays? The focus was on Scottish youth as, by this time, Pearl had joined the department for Social and Economic Research at the University of Glasgow. Funded by Calouste Gulbenkian Foundation on the Bellahouston Bequest Fund, as well as the Scottish department for education, *A Time of One's Own* is a detailed study of 600 adolescents aged 15 to 19 in three areas of Scotland – Armadale, Dennistoun and Drumchapel. Methodologically creative and eclectic, Pearl drew upon discussions, observations, and diaries and visited young people in homes, churches, youth organisations and at their places of work. Another standout feature of the text, typical of Pearl's imagination and creativity, was the use of art, sketches, maps, photographs etc., that were used as analytical material. Pearl commissioned artists to draw or paint young people at leisure as she felt artists might see something different in the world from what the social research may observe. Such creativity makes this book very different from a standard sociological report on young people at the time. Instead, it speaks very much to Pearl's desire to access and understand the social world around her via any possible means. To that end, the book is not only a study of how young people in Scotland spent their leisure time in the 1960s but is also an example of how one can research the creative, imaginative possibilities that sociology offers.

An extensive archive of material housed at the University of Glasgow Archives survive under this text, alongside materials that Pearl collected for the study and her other 'Scottish' book, *Homes in High Flats*. Archive materials include the additional images and photographs taken by Pearl and the supplementary artwork she commissioned. The Archives are a veritable treasure trove for any social scientist interested in the history of our discipline and craft.

I will end with one question. How can a researcher in her 60s, born in England in 1900 with a grammar school and university education, access the ordinary lives of young Scottish people? The answer to the question is in the book and the other pieces written about Pearl. Pearl Jephcott had 'no side' and no political agenda and was clearly able to make people feel at ease using various research tools to capture their thoughts and feelings. These are rare skills that many researchers never fully develop or deploy that well. Perhaps it was Pearl's early career as a youth worker and the ingrained empathy and approachability that made Pearl such a successful sociologist in her later life. As such, for any would-be sociologist the advice has to be – be more like Pearl, aspire to be creative, try to be imaginative, and most importantly, empathise with the 'other' to reduce the distance between you as the researcher and those being researched.

John Goodwin
University of Leicester
October 2022

TIME OF ONE'S OWN

Leisure and Young People

PEARL JEPHCOTT
Department of Social and Economic Research
University of Glasgow

University of Glasgow Social and Economic Studies
Occasional Papers No. 7

OLIVER & BOYD
EDINBURGH AND LONDON

OLIVER AND BOYD LTD
Tweeddale Court
Edinburgh 1
39A Welbeck Street
London W1

First published 1967

© 1967 Pearl Jephcott

Printed in Great Britain by
Robert Cunningham and Sons Ltd, Alva

ACKNOWLEDGMENTS

Thanks are due to those individuals and institutions who initiated the study. Grateful acknowledgment of financial aid must be given to the Calouste Gulbenkian Foundation and the Bellahouston Bequest Fund. The Scottish Education Department supported the work with both funds and counsel. A special debt is owed to those who gave time and ability to locating and interviewing 600 adolescents, and also to the devisers of this sample of the 15-19 population in the three areas where the study was undertaken—Armadale, Dennistoun and Drumchapel. Others to be thanked include the adults who recorded the talk at youngsters' discussion groups, arranged for batches of young people to write down their views, and induced individual ones to keep diaries. Numerous churches, firms, educational institutions and youth organisations furthered the work, and here particular mention should be made of the secondary schools in the above three study areas. A different type of help was given by those who collected informed opinion from the adult residents of these areas about the recreational needs of the local youngsters. Other helpers kindly made sketches, drew maps, took photographs, read drafts and checked figures. Special mention must be made of the work on young people's reading undertaken by Mrs D. J. Robertson. The study in general and the statistical material in particular owes much to Mr Iain Cameron; the secretarial work to Miss E. Fairgrieve. The warmest thanks of all go to the 3,000 or so boys and girls who, in one way or another, gave their co-operation. It would be good to think that they and their leisure will be

> Blest with all that Heav'n can send,
> Long Youth, long Pleasure and a Friend.

Team of Voluntary Interviewers

Miss M. Auld (School Welfare Officer); Mr W. Burrows (Boys' Brigade Officer); Miss E. Campbell (Health Visitor); Mr T. Carruthers (Lecturer in Psychology); Miss D. Clucas (School Welfare Officer); Miss A. Cockburn (Secretary); Mr J. Craig

(Lecturer in Economics); Miss J. Donaldson (Nurse); Miss J. Ellor (Teacher); Mr J. Good (Lecturer in Social Psychology); Mrs E. Gryza (Speech Therapist); Mrs E. Haluch (County Councillor); Mr R. Harris (Education and Training Officer); Miss A. Jamieson (Nurse); Miss M. McCawley (Teacher); Miss A. MacDougall (Teacher); Mr A. McFarlane (Personnel Manager); Miss J. McGarry (Adviser to Women Students); Miss L. Mackenzie (Health Visitor); Miss C. McLean (Secretary); Mr W. D. McLean (Marriage Guidance Counsellor); Mr C. Morris (Lecturer in English and Social Studies); Mr M. Murray (Teacher); Miss C. Nowrie (Secretary); Mr R. Nummey (Welfare Officer); Miss M. Pender (School Welfare Officer); Mr R. Purves (After-Care Officer for Approved Schools); Mr W. Rhind (Boys' Brigade Officer); Mr J. Round (Tutor in Youth Leadership); Mrs M. Scott (Housewife); Mr D. Smith (Welfare Officer); Mr R. Smith (Personnel Manager); Miss G. Swan (Health Visitor); Mr A. Thomson (Personnel Manager); Mr I. Thomson (Lecturer in Physical Education); Mrs M. Torbet (School Welfare Officer); Mrs A. Watson (Marriage Guidance Counsellor); Miss A. Welsh (Health Visitor); Mr R. Winter (Welfare Officer); Miss M. Young (Health Visitor).

Field Work Team

Miss S. Bayne (Art Teacher); Miss U. Gordon (Art Teacher); Mr D. Gower (Student, Glasgow University School of Social Study); Mr I. Love (Student, Glasgow School of Art); Mr J. Morris (Student, Jordanhill College of Education, Youth Leadership Course); Mr B. Nesbitt (Student, Glasgow University School of Social Study).

Illustrations

Miss U. Gordon I, III, VII; Miss S. Bayne 7, 9, 14; Mr I. Love 3, 4, 11, 15; Various boys and girls (age 14 and 15) 5, 6, 8, 10, 12, 13.

SUBJECT AND SETTING

Requested by The Standing Consultative Council on Youth and Community Service. Chairman: Lord Kilbrandon.

Undertaken by Miss P. Jephcott, Department of Social and Economic Research, The University of Glasgow (Professor D. J. Robertson).

Subject A study in three areas on how those aged 15-19 spend their free time.

Date January 1964-June 1966 (preceded by three months' work on background information).

Estimated population (1964) aged 15-19
    Drumchapel 5,600 (16% of total population)
    Dennistoun 1,500 (6·7% of total population)
    Armadale 550 (8·8% of total population)

Number of adolescents (aged 15-19) from whom information was obtained

Interviewed	600
Consulted through pilot interviews, discussion groups and Leavers (approx.)	800
Consulted through written work (approx.)	1,600
Total	3,000

Personnel Voluntary interviewers and field work team—see 'Acknowledgments'.
University staff
Miss P. Jephcott January 1964-June 1966
Mr I. Cameron October 1963-July 1965
Mr B. Nesbitt September 1965-March 1966 (part-time)

CONTENTS

	Acknowledgments	v
	Subject and Setting	vii
	Illustrations	x
	List of Tables	xi
I	The Purpose of the Study	1
II	Leisure and Young People	10
III	The Three Areas Selected for Study	18
IV	Methods	32
V	The Facts—as Shown in Interviews with a Sample of the 15-19 Age Group in Three Areas	46
	Introduction	46
	The adolescents' background	48
	Leisure spent at home	57
	Leisure I (Casual leisure other than that spent at home)	64
	Leisure II (Cinema, dancing, cafe, etc.)	68
VI	Some of the Views Expressed by the Boys and Girls	83
VII	Conclusions	102
	Appendices	
	A. Nature and validity of material derived through interviews	150
	B. Glasgow Education Authority:	
	I. Recreation and informal education centres 1964-65	154
	II. Assistance given by Authority during the financial year 1964-65	155
	C. Tables	156

ILLUSTRATIONS

HALF-TONE PLATES

I	Some of the boys and girls	*Frontispiece*
II	Female coal-bearers in Scotland in the 1840's	
III	Cafe life, Armadale	
IV	Dennistoun	
V	Drumchapel	Between
VI	Some of the girls, Drumchapel	pp. 68 & 69
VII	At the bus stop, Armadale	
VIII	Close-up, Drumchapel	
IX	Armadale	

MAPS AND LINE DRAWINGS

1	Central Scotland—Study areas	4
2	Glasgow—Study areas	5
3	Boys' Brigade, Dennistoun	11
4	Leisure at home, Dennistoun	21
5	'A really enjoyable Saturday' as described by three school children aged 14-15	36
6	Motorbike owner	44
7	Boys, aged 16-17, unloading a lorry	54
8	Service?	67
9	Club art class, Drumchapel	79
10	'Trouble'	93
11	Club dancing class, Dennistoun	103
12	Football	111
13	'Going to the pictures'	121
14	Nowhere to go	132
15	Band class, Dennistoun	146

LIST OF TABLES*

1	Composition of sample in relation to sex, age and current educational situation	47
	Composition of sample in relation to age groups (%)	47
	Composition of sample in relation to current educational situation (%)	47
2	Composition of sample in relation to area and age (%)	48
3	Number of people living in home in relation to educational situation of adolescent (%)	156
4	Nature of father's job in relation to educational situation of adolescent (%)	156
	Nature of father's job in relation to full-time education of adolescent (summary)	156
5	Nature of mother's work situation in relation to area (%)	157
6	Type of school or college being attended (by those who are still in full-time education)(%)	157
	Type of school or college last attended (by those who have left full-time education) (%)	157
7	Age at leaving full-time education (%)	157
8	Attendance (current and previous) at further education class or training school (%)	157
9A	Type of current job in relation to type or types of leisure participated in (%)	158
9B	Type of current job in relation to area (%)	159
10	Number of jobs held in relation to age (%)	160
11	Last week's take-home pay in relation to age and sex (%)	160
12	Last week's spending money in relation to age and sex (%)	160
13	Smoking costs per week in relation to age and sex (%)	160
14	'How did you spend yesterday evening?' (%)	161
15	'How did you spend the summer (1964) holidays?' (%)	161
16	'Do you read a daily newspaper?' (%)	162
17	'What kind of magazines do you see regularly?' (%)	162
18	'Do you read books?' (in relation to current educational situation) (%)	162
19	Participation in Leisure Activities I in relation to sex, age and educational situation (%)	163
20	Participation in Leisure Activities I during last 7 days (%)	163
21	Visit to (a) cafe (b) pub during last 7 days in relation to area (%)	164
22	Participation in Leisure Activities II in relation to sex, age and educational situation (%)	164

23	Participation in Leisure Activities II during last 7 days (%)	164
24	Membership of formal group in relation to sex, age and educational situation (%)	165
25	Attendance (by whole sample) at a formal group during last 7 days (%)	165

* Additional tables and fuller versions of certain of those listed above may be seen on application to the Department of Social and Economic Research, The University, Glasgow.

Chapter I

THE PURPOSE OF THE STUDY

How do young Scots use their free time nowadays? This study tried to find some of the answers to the above question. It explored, for example, the facts and feelings which lay behind a typical comment made by the 15-year-old girl who wrote:

In our district there is no entertainment. There is only a couple of dance halls and they have a bad name. We have to travel for pictures or to go swimming. At night girls and boys just walk about the streets and hope for the best. We just go about with boys and have a carry on. Even then there is too much police about.

Again, what accounted for the following views, this time from a 17-year-old boy? Asked, were he an M.P., what he would do for the benefit of himself and his friends as regards their leisure, he made the following suggestions:

1. Provide easier access to skiing areas and make skiing cheaper.
2. Attempt to remove the shady stigma of billiards and snooker.
3. Later closings for cinemas and some dance halls.
4. Provide better entertainment at coastal towns during summer and more entertainment in Glasgow suburbs.
5. Later closings for pubs and licensed restaurants all over Glasgow not just city centre establishments.
6. Lower hire purchase age limit on some commodities (clothes, cars, record players, tape recorders).
7. Allow teenagers to have their own choice of schoolwear and personal clothes, not governed by teachers or parents.
8. Have more interesting subjects for study in English i.e. modern novels and magazines.

A more robust and imaginative provision for young people's leisure was among the many plans made in the early post-war years. The magnitude of the 1944-9 birth rate also focused attention on to the needs of the rising generation. In Scotland, as in Britain, there was much dissatisfaction with the Youth Service, the official agency for worthwhile opportunities for young people's free time. Crippled by shortage of funds and trained personnel, the Service also lacked any agreed policy between the statutory and the voluntary sides of its work.

There was an uneasy suspicion that the existing Service was not geared to the current needs and aspirations of the younger generation, particularly those of adolescent age. Various official bodies were asking questions about the Service throughout the 1950's and 60's.[1] The outcome of all this discussion was that, in 1959, the Secretary of State for Scotland set up a Standing Consultative Council on Youth Service in Scotland—the Kilbrandon Council.

A few years later, in 1964, one of the Council's many activities was to initiate two research projects on how Scotland's 420,000 boys and girls of 15-19 used their spare time now that leisure is becoming less a footnote to work than important in its own right. Examination of the evidence might help explode stock generalisations based on hear-say and prejudice. The first project, and that with which this report deals, was a fact-finding one on how young people in Scotland spend their leisure. The second was a piece of operational research into the leisure-time needs of a particular section of youngsters, those making no use of the facilities provided by the Youth Service. The Department of Social and Economic Research of the University of Glasgow was asked to undertake the first of these studies, the Scottish Standing Conference of Voluntary Youth Organisations to direct the second. Both were financed by the Scottish Education Department assisted in the case of the University study by grants from the Calouste Gulbenkian Foundation and the Bellahouston Bequest.

The original terms of reference of the University fact finding study were as follows:

The object of the enquiry is to describe and evaluate the leisure-time interests and social attitudes of young people in Scotland. It will be particu-

[1] Advisory Council on Education in Scotland—*Report* 1952; Advisory Committee of the Association of Directors of Education—*Report on the Youth Service* 1956; Scottish Leadership Training Association, Conference 1957; *15-18 Report of the Central Advisory Council for Education*—England (Crowther Report), H.M.S.O. 1959; *The Youth Service in England and Wales* (Albermarle Report), H.M.S.O. 1959; *Sport in the Community* (Wolfenden Report), Central Council of Physical Recreation 1960; *Training of Part-time Youth Leaders and Assistants* (Bessey Report), Ministry of Education H.M.S.O. 1962; *Half our Future* (Newsom Report), Central Advisory Council for Education, England H.M.S.O. 1963; *From School to Further Education* (Brunton Report), Scottish Education Department, H.M.S.O. 1963; *Day Release* (Henniker-Heaton Report), Department of Education and Science, H.M.S.O. 1964.

larly concerned with the middle group of critical and non-conforming young people who remain unaffected by organised youth activities and at the same time avoid becoming part of the delinquent or actively anti-social minority. The enquiry will be conducted in such a way as to provide an assessment both of the potentialities for worthwhile future development in youth service provision and of the limitations of existing provision particularly in relation to the young people who do not at present participate in its work and who might be benefited by it.

Points to note are that the study was to concern itself primarily with the 'middle group' of young people, the ordinary youngster who, while making his own recreations without resource to formal youth groups, does not get involved in official trouble. Just what these adolescents did with their free time was to be explored and some attempt was to be made to assess its quality. It was hoped that the findings would indicate certain of the broad principles which should govern today's provision for leisure.

'Young people in Scotland' proved too wide a range for the resources available and the study had to be narrowed as regards age and area. The age was limited to those aged 15-19, partly on the ground that this is a convenient grouping statistically but also because 15 and 19 are recognised boundaries in that the great majority make the vital transition from school to work at 15, while at 19 the fact that they are about to drop the word 'teen' supports them in their image of themselves as adults. The 15-19 age group of this study was, of course, the generation born in the early post-war years. It is often difficult for adults to realise just how unfamiliar today's adolescents may be with the recent past. An example met with was a conversation in which one 16-year-old, asking another 'What were the S.S. men then?' received the reply 'Something to do with sex wasn't it?' It may help to place the youngsters of this study on the more immediate time-scale if one mentions that, as far as the girls are concerned, beehive hair styles were 'in' when the study started and mini-skirts as yet unknown by the date it ended. As regards area, Scotland was found to be too large and too diverse for the resources available. Even if a suitable methodology could have been devised, leisure-time needs and facilities in remote rural areas differ radically from those of the industrial belt of the Central Lowlands. Since this belt contains two-thirds of the population it was decided to concentrate the work there and three small localities within it

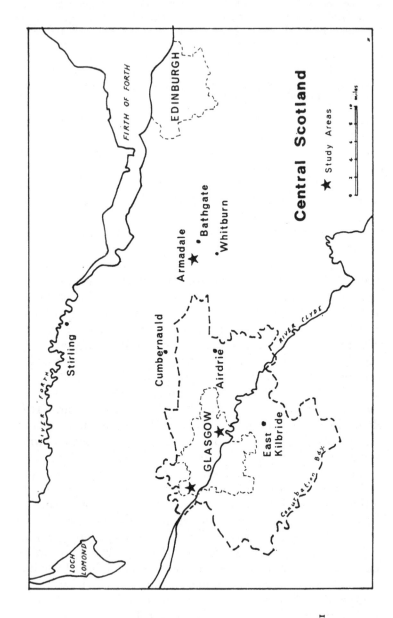

Fig. 1

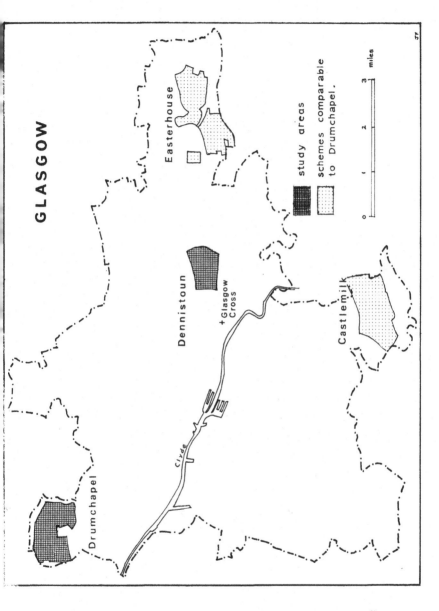

FIG. 2

AGE GROUPS

Scotland, Glasgow, West Lothian and three study areas (figures from Census 1961 and from Registrar-General's Annual Estimates at June, 1961)

AREAS

AGE GROUP	SCOTLAND	GLASGOW	WEST LOTHIAN	DENNISTOUN	DRUMCHAPEL	ARMADALE
0–4 (1961)	469,200—9·05%	101,338—9·61%	8,824—9·52%	2,154—9·27%	3,187—9·05%	554—8·94%
15–19 (1961)	373,900—7·2%	79,756—7·57%	7,100—7·65%	1,505—6·49%	3,626—10·3%	458—7·4%
65 and over (1961)	545,600—10·52%	99,029—9·38%	8,320—8·96%	2,743—11·82%	921—2·6%	512—8·27%
15–19 (1964)*	426,500—8·22%	87,220—8·27%	8,168—8·8%	1,564—6·75%	5,656—16·07%	548—8·84%
TOTAL POPULATION (1961)	5,183,900	1,055,017	92,768	23,277	35,182	6,195

* Projection based on 1961 figures for the 12–16 age group.

were eventually chosen for study. Selected less for comparative purposes than because they were thought to have numerous counterparts in Central Scotland, they were as follows: a ten-year-old housing estate on the north-west of Glasgow (Drumchapel—estimated 1964 population 40,000), an old inner-urban district of Glasgow (Dennistoun—estimated population 25,000), and a small but expanding industrial town in West Lothian (Armadale—estimated neighbourhood population 8,000). The 15-19 age group of the areas was estimated at 5,600, 1,500 and 550 respectively. Thus the two Glasgow areas contained 7,000, or rather less than a twelfth of the city's 87,000 adolescents, and Armadale had 550, or about a fifteenth of the 8,000 boys and girls aged 15-19 in West Lothian.

The funds permitted the appointment to the staff of the University of a senior research officer and an assistant. The former did field work for two-and-a-half years, the latter for two years. The major initial task, that of interviewing a sample of the 15-19 age group in each of the three areas, was undertaken by some 43 voluntary helpers, men and women of all ages and engaged in a variety of professions. They themselves devised the schedule used for the interviews and held numerous small meetings during the course of their work. In a good many cases they continued to be consulted about the study throughout its whole course. A generous contingencies allowance made it possible to enlist additional helpers of another kind for short-term pieces of field work. Most of the six young men and women engaged on this were in their early twenties and thus not so far removed from their own adolescence. Their work brought them into casual contact with youngsters in cafes, pubs, youth groups, dance halls, etc., as well as in private houses. The study owed an immense amount to the goodwill, competence, and sheer hard work of the above fifty or so helpers. That so many people in full-time jobs were prepared to undertake this work indicates the concern, in the Quaker sense, felt by Scottish society for its younger members. It also suggests a lively awareness of all the new opportunities which increased leisure affords.

The team held 123 pilot interviews on a preliminary schedule in areas adjacent to those where the sample proper was to be used. They asked for, and in most cases obtained, an interview with every boy and girl aged 15-19 living at a random sample of addresses in the above three areas (Appendix A). The original schedule was much modified in the light of the experience gained at this pilot stage. In the main sample itself 600 interviews were completed and the material from them analysed statistically. They were held under a variety of conditions, the majority taking place in the adolescent's own home. Though a certain amount of background information was asked on his family, education and job, most of the interview was spent in establishing the facts about the what, when and how of his leisure.

As soon as the interviews were finished the work turned to obtaining young people's opinions on why they spent their free time as they did. Although this second type of material was not confined to the youngsters of the three areas, practically all of it came either from various parts of Glasgow or from the Armadale/Bathgate locality. As in the case of the interviews, the age of those consulted was kept strictly to 15-19. One source of information was 76 informal and quite small discussion groups on leisure. About 600 adolescents took part in these, meeting at firms, technical colleges, youth groups and private houses. In general only one adult was present, his business being to start the ball rolling, fade into the background and record the substance of the talk. Typical notes, from a discussion group of 7 girls and 3 boys aged about 17 (shop, factory, office and school) read as follows:

Almost no use is made of organised youth services by this group. The services provided just aren't what is wanted. Week-ends are good as regards leisure but very little is done during the week. Most stay in an average of three nights a week but the extremes here were from one night to six nights. When they go out during the week they don't do anything special. (A direct question on attitudes to authority brought little response.) One or two of the group had had probation officers and viewed these as 'nosey' but easy to kid on. On police there were the usual denigratory epithets but again they felt that the police were necessary and more of them were needed. Only two police to patrol Drumchapel at nights. On teachers, most of the group now realise that their teachers weren't so bad and can now understand their attitude; but this was not universal. The clergy trouble some consciences but the effect is short-lived and some don't feel troubled at all.

Written, as distinct from verbal, views were obtained by asking other adolescents for their confidential opinions on certain topics connected broadly with their leisure. Most of this type of material, provided by about 1,600 youngsters, was obtained through the help of educational institutions of many kinds; a smaller amount came from groups connected with churches, firms, 'Homes', approved schools, youth organisations, etc. Additional written comment was provided by 17 boys and girls who kept brief records of their leisure over a short period.

Another method by which information was collected direct from the adolescents of the study areas was by getting a few adults to keep fairly close contact with a small number of boys and girls from their 15th to 17th birthdays. The 40 youngsters in question were first met in the spring of 1964, the introductions being through secondary schools, one in each of the three areas. The schools chose these 40 more or less at random from among their 15-year-old Easter leavers. Subsequent contact between team member and adolescent was made wherever convenient, most of it taking place at the youngster's home. Only three adults were concerned with the leavers and in some cases a fairly close relationship was built up. Notes made after a typical contact read:

Had a brief chat to T.'s mother when I first called.... The house from what I could see by just standing at the doorway looked very poor and dirty.... Found T. perfectly happy to chat on the stairway. She said she spent most of her time going to a cafe in —— where her boy friend worked, or listening to records or, more recently, going bus-runs organised by this cafe. Seems to have no want of friends and gets on well with her mates.... At present she is a cashier at ——. Her job causes her to move around quite a bit.... Her hours are 9.00 a.m. till 6.30 p.m. She does not like her present job and thinks she may well change it soon.... She also mentioned the fact that she was offered a part-time job at the cafe she frequented. However her boy friend would not let her take it, but her mother would like it and was going to write to the man who owns the cafe.

In exploring the how and why of the youngster's leisure one experimental method tried was to get young professional artists to make sketches of how the adolescents in the three areas were spending their after-work hours. This technique was used on the assumption that the artist sees that much deeper than the man in the street. These sketches, together with certain ones produced by boys and girls aged 14 and 15 suggested that the adolescents of the three areas were far less uniform than is implied by the blanketing and vaguely denigratory image evoked by the word 'teenager'.

Chapter II

LEISURE AND YOUNG PEOPLE

The immediate reasons for this study have been referred to earlier. More far-reaching ones are linked with certain broad changes which have taken place in society during the last fifty years. The extension in the amount of leisure which the individual now has at his disposal is one of the most significant of such changes. An interesting shift has taken place in the common usage of the word. Traditionally, as in the Bible's apposition of 'labour' and 'rest', leisure has been regarded primarily as a period of inaction after the physical toil involved in earning one's daily bread. This concept is being replaced by a more positive one which is closer to the word's true meaning. As defined by the O.E.D. leisure is 'the opportunity afforded by unoccupied time' and 'the freedom ... to do something'. Both have a positive tang about them which is missing from the traditional use of the word. Since any extension of the leisure in one's life is basically an extension in personal liberty, leisure should take its place alongside, and may be as revolutionary as the new freedoms provided by such things as better health or the more equitable distribution of wealth. Other important changes relating to leisure mean that all sections of society now have access to what in the past was the prerogative of a tiny minority. Spending on leisure, too, is no longer such a criterion of class distinction as used to be the case.[1] Women in particular have scored as regards the increase in leisure. Fewer pregnancies, smaller families and an earlier cessation in child-bearing (made possible by the increased knowledge and efficiency of contraceptives) mean that a smaller proportion of woman's life is engrossed in the essential biological work which child-bearing and rearing entails. Science and technology have lightened the housewife's load as well as being immensely influential in wider fields.

Work in general is infinitely less laborious than man has ever known it in the past. Two examples of the physical effort that

[1] *Leisure in America.* Kaplan. Wiley, 1960.

the day's work might entail even for a youngster are as follows. Though both refer to as long ago as the early nineteenth century the association of work with physical toil has continued until fairly recent times. The first example relates to Livingstone's job as an adolescent of the 1820's in the Blantyre mill. The machinery was mostly manually operated and the hours were from 6.00 a.m. to 8.00 p.m. with only short breaks for meals.

Fig. 3. Boys' Brigade, Dennistoun

Young workers there were required by the employer to attend evening classes every night from 8.00 to 10.00 p.m.[2] The Scottish girl miner's job of a couple of decades later appeared to be even more laborious if one can judge from a contemporary account.[3] (See Plate II facing p. 68).

> The mother, having thus disposed of her younger children, descends the pit with her older daughters, when each, having a basket of a suitable form, lays it down, and into it the large coals are rolled; and such is the weight carried, that it frequently takes two men to lift the burden upon their backs: the girls are loaded according to their strength. The mother sets out first, carrying a lighted candle in her teeth; the girls follow, and in this manner they proceed to the pit bottom, and with weary steps and slow, ascend the stairs, halting occasionally to draw breath, till they arrive at the hill or pit-top, where the coals are laid down for sale; and in this manner they go for eight or ten hours almost without resting.

Less physical effort demanded by the day's work added to improvement in health means that more energy is available for non-working hours than was the case when the manual (and typical) worker was driven to use his limited leisure for physical recuperation if he was to be fit enough to earn the following day. The fact that even today about half the national labour force is engaged in manual labour suggests why the traditional views about leisure remain so entrenched. It also helps to explain why inaction during one's free hours is still mostly shrugged off as very understandable, whereas idleness as regards working hours has always been looked on as a bad trait of character and a loss to society. That pleasure as such is something which ought to be provided for is a fairly new conception. The traditional, accepted outlook on leisure was frequently encountered in the course of this study. Many parents adopted a highly permissive attitude about their adolescent child's use of his leisure—'He does what he likes in his own time.'

Another change in the nature of leisure is that its extension is not confined to a larger daily and yearly dose so to speak. Leisure now permeates the whole span of life in that there is

---

[2] Information kindly supplied by the Warden, Livingstone Memorial, Blantyre.

[3] 'Inquiry into the Condition of Women who carry Coals under Ground in Scotland, known by the name of Bearers (Edinburgh, 1812)', *Human Documents of the Industrial Revolution in Britain*. Royston Pike. Allen and Unwin, 1966.

additional leisure, in the sense of more years spent in compulsory education rather than the paid job, at the beginning of life; while earlier retirement, together with an increased life expectancy, provides a longer spell of non-working years towards life's end. Typical examples of people still living who had undergone this restricted leisure as children were two elderly men met with in Armadale both of whom had started full-time work in a pit when they were eleven. Another characteristic of leisure nowadays is that the main breaks with work are tending to be concentrated rather than spread evenly over the week and the year. The long week-end is a case in point; so is today's preference for four days on a 10-hour shift rather than an 8-hour shift for five days. The trend towards shift work, too, means that leisure becomes available at times and seasons that are not the familiar ones. A free week-day morning, the result of increasing flexibility in shop hours, may replace the traditional early closing afternoon. Some of the youngsters of this study were beginning to get an annual winter holiday in addition to the summer one. A rapid spread of longer annual holidays is envisaged, especially if Britain enters the European Economic Community.[4] On the whole, however, the significant change probably relates less to shorter hours than to new patterns in the times and seasons when leisure is available.

Another interesting alteration in the character of leisure is that the old distinction between work and play is becoming less clear-cut.[5] Jobs are increasingly concerned with people rather than things, and people and their concerns are less readily dismissed from mind at the end of the day than are 'things'. The typical club girl of the 1930's, the factory girl, spent her working hours in a way that was quite foreign to her non-working ones. Today's hairdresser's assistant, or the girl in the supermarket, spends her 9-5 hours in a world that may not be all that dissimilar to the rest of her day. The range of ways in which leisure can now be spent has, of course, grown enormously. Increased spending power has been a major factor here. As any unemployed man knew only too well in the depression years of the 1930's, leisure lost its savour when poverty grossly restricted his possibility of choice. The writer noted the same outlook on leisure among the many unemployed

[4] *Fringe Benefits. Labour Costs and Social Security.* Reid and Robertson. Allen and Unwin, 1965. [5] *op. cit.* Kaplan.

adolescents of the West Indies. Improved communications have multiplied the range of places, and the weakening of social class barriers has broadened the company, in which leisure can be spent. Mass media communications have been very influential in drawing attention to unfamiliar ways of using the extra time now available. In general there is a trend towards more variety in the types of activity pursued, but more uniformity about the activity itself. An example is the decline in attendance at professional football matches, a leisure-time activity that arose to meet the needs of large urban populations with limited time and money and a new legal right to a free Saturday afternoon. Watching football is to some extent now being replaced by participation in, or watching, a host of other sports. The classic example of uniformity connected with one type of activity is T.V., where millions occupy an identical part of their leisure time in an identical way.

Increased spending power has, of course, been a major influence in widening the uses to which free time can be put, and commercial enterprise has seized on these new markets. At the simplest level it caters for the demand for that bit of immediate solo pleasure—a cigarette, an ice lolly—which is part of leisure's image. It also trades on the need to fill up time by providing home-based activities like football pools, competitions, and the do-it-yourself movement. Light reading, the three or four Sunday papers and the women's magazines which get into pretty well every home, represents another way in which commercial enterprise cashes in on the demands produced by the happy combination of more free time and more spare cash. Commercial enterprise also caters for that increase in informal social contacts which shorter working hours make possible. Facilities for companionable talk and drinking have increased greatly, not only through changes in the social character of pubs but in new provision in the shape of cafes and milk bars. Today's extensive use of cafes by working-class women and by adolescents is closely related to the increase in leisure. As soon as one filler-up-of-leisure stales, another is thought up, as in the translation of cinemas into bingo halls and an old pastime like skittles into ten-pin bowling.

Certain of the many changes which have so radically affected society since the turn of the century have been intensified in the case of the younger generation. In bodily growth, for example, children have had more than their fair share of the general improvement. One Glasgow sample showed that the average height of children at five years old increased by 2 in. over the past 50 years and that the children were 3 lb. heavier in weight.[6] Today's 12-year-old is the physical counterpart of the 13-year-old of 15 years ago. Nor have adults had a parallel gain to that which longer schooling has given the younger ages. As said earlier, any lengthening of full-time education can be regarded as an extension of leisure since the school child or student has fewer externally imposed limitations on his time than is the case with the young worker. What 16-year-old working-class boy of the past would have been able to sit in a cafe 'with the crowd' on seven occasions in one week (as did the schoolboy writer of one of the diaries kept for this study)? Affluence, too, has directly eased the lot of the younger generation in that they are no longer required to spend their time and labour on eking out the family income, a common enough situation in the past. As regards earnings from full-time work, the adolescent has improved his position more than has the adult. Between 1951 and 1962 juvenile weekly wage rates in the U.K. rose by 83% compared with a 69% rise for all workers. Earnings probably bear more closely on how adolescents use their leisure than they do with adults since a youngster's wages represents money that is relatively uncommitted. Another of the alterations in social life which has been so to speak magnified in the case of the adolescent is the trend towards earlier marriage. A much larger proportion of those still in their teens now enjoy the status which marriage confers than was the case before 1931 when the downward spiral began. All told, therefore, the adolescent exercises considerably more power now than formerly, while improved physique, a smarter appearance and longer education mean that he is more articulate and can communicate better with adults in all classes of society and hold his own at an earlier age with them. Young people's considered questioning of adult authority at one end of the scale, and the increase in juvenile delinquency at the other, can both be regarded as manifestations of strained relationships arising from the new powers wielded by those still in their teens. One indication of these changes in the last

[6] 'The Young Child', Mathews. *The Principles of Health Visiting*. ed. Cunningham. Faber, 1967.

decade is, of course, the growth of a distinctive youth culture. Even to be looked on as being crazy is all part of the game of being an adolescent.

Another of the more general reasons for this study was a widespread disquiet about certain of the values to which adolescents are said to subscribe. Though not necessarily suspect, many of these values are unfamiliar. Respect for authority as represented by church, school, parents and police was certainly not accepted uncritically by most of the youngsters of this study. Ministers were brushed off as talking 'about things that happened thousands of years ago'; or 'Adults don't *know*—they live in an old world'; or 'We'd rather learn the hard way than believe or do what older people tell us.' Another unfamiliar value was that so many youngsters, including girls, regarded drinking as an essential component of enjoying one's leisure. Parties were dead unless there was drink galore and a considerable quantity of drink was regularly smuggled into dances attended chiefly by those still in their mid-teens. Trouble, physical violence in particular, appeared to be accepted as an almost inevitable accompaniment of adolescent life.[7] The phrases used time and again referred to 'those who turn to violence for pleasure', 'to 'the amount of violence and vandalism in my district', and to youngsters who 'just roam the streets making gangs and creating havoc'. In so far as a permissive attitude to pre-marital intercourse was openly expressed this again appeared to be a new outlook—'Some do, some don't, it's up to you.'

Other anxieties were associated with how these young men and women on the fringe of adult life were making use of their leisure. The dangers of 'precious time mis-spent' become all the more obvious as the number of hours within one's own control increases. Many misgivings were expressed about the current state of the Youth Service, that combination of statutory and voluntary provision for young people's leisure which presupposes the presentation of certain values which society deems important. Much thought and public money have been expended on the Service in the last decade and its quality has undoubtedly improved, but no corresponding increase in the extent to which the 15-19 age group makes use of the Service

[7] 'Trouble' with a capital T is used throughout this report when referring to anti-social behaviour in general.

appears to be taking place. Reliable comparative figures are almost impossible to come by but non-users within this age group undoubtedly still outnumber users and, very important, those whose educational and social needs are most pressing appear to use the Service least. It is a case of 'to him that hath'. Why more youngsters do not take advantage of the Youth Service remains the oddly intractable problem which it has always been.

To recapitulate. Assuming that an increase in leisure represents an extension in personal freedom, society plainly has an obligation to prepare its younger members for the new opportunities to hand. Guidance is particularly necessary for this current generation of adolescents since they are almost certainly being subjected to more strains than were their predecessors. They have, for example, experienced in an exaggerated form certain of the changes which have taken place in society as a whole since the turn of the century. Improved health, affluence, longer education, less arduous working conditions and earlier marriage have endowed them with increased powers, and the field in which they can most readily exercise these is, of course, their free time. While the Youth Service is certainly not the sole, and probably not even the major solution to the opportunities made available by increased leisure, experience shows that it can be very influential both in a locality and on the individual youngster. If some schools of thought still question the case for the Service and for what is sometimes regarded as undue meddling with young people's own affairs, one matter is not in dispute. There is going to be a considerable rise in the 15-19 population in the decade immediately ahead (1969-79) and, by implication, an increase in the existing opportunities and problems posed by adolescents and their free time.

CHAPTER III

THE THREE AREAS SELECTED FOR STUDY

The areas selected for study differed markedly in their physical appearance and social character. Dennistoun is thought to be fairly typical of Glasgow's long settled inner urban areas, Drumchapel of the city's major post-war housing estates, and Armadale of the many coal and ore mining townships (Whitburn, Shotts, Broxburn etc.) which grew up in West Lothian during the nineteenth century. In Armadale, mining has now been replaced by general industrial work. Dennistoun, on the eastern side of Glasgow, is within a mile of such time-honoured focal points as the Saltmarket, the Cathedral and Toll Cross. By contrast Drumchapel, 7 miles west of the city centre, is on the edge of open country and has for its northern backcloth the ridge of hills along which the Antonine Wall drops down to the Clyde. Armadale, 20 miles east of Glasgow, is strung along the old coach road to Edinburgh. Lying high, it has distant views of the Grampians and Ochil Hills and nearer ones of a thin-looking farmland studded with pit workings and rust-coloured bings.

Dennistoun has a population of about 23,000 which makes it roughly comparable in size with such a town as Dumbarton. The northern and southern boundaries of that main part of the ward which comprised the study area are two busy thoroughfares.[1] The first of those, Alexandra Parade, is any arterial road emerging from a city centre—straight, wide, treeless and traffic-laden. Blocks of shops topped by tenements are interspersed with industrial buildings, garages and hoardings. North of the Parade is a steep hillside scarred with derelict works, disused railway lines and a live gas works. Further to the east but still on this sloping terrain is one of Glasgow's fine and well-kept parks. The southern boundary is Duke Street which is lined with shops that cater for a mainly artisan population. Running south from Duke Street are streets of tall

[1] The north-west corner of the ward was excluded as being somewhat cut off from what is generally regarded as Dennistoun.

tenements. These cut across a network of railway lines and extend to the old crowded district of Gallowgate. As far as Duke Street is concerned, industrial Glasgow flows on for another 2 miles without much change of character.

Dennistoun ward, part of which includes the hillside mentioned above, is nearly 700 acres in size. Roughly rectangular, it extends rather over half a mile from east to west and also from north to south. At the date of the study the 15-19 age group was estimated as about 1,500, or 6·7% of the total population. Thus the proportion of adolescents is only slightly below that found in any 'normal' population. Dennistoun's 8,000 private households live in very varied types of building and there are sizable localities and even streets which show marked social contrasts. A small area of pleasant Edwardian villas at the western end is now partly occupied by hotels and offices. Towards the east is a much larger district of shabby, inter-war council flats interspersed with industrial premises. Twenty-eight per cent of all Dennistoun households live in council-owned property. Between these two flanks are straight streets of 4-storey red sandstone tenements, some rented but an increasing number now owner-occupied. These, the core of Dennistoun, account for its popular image as stable, old-established, lower middle-class locality living on modest but steady incomes. Figures from the sample interviews suggested one or two points about Dennistoun's social character. There was a high proportion of small (3 person) households. Nearly half the sample adolescents had a father in non-manual work, which was twice the proportion for the other two study areas both of which are solidly working class.

Dennistoun has good local facilities for education and is so centrally situated that it has easy access to many other of the city's educational institutions. There are three secondary schools actually within the ward or on its immediate boundaries. If the information from the interviews was typical, well over half the 15-19 population has had its secondary education at one or other of Dennistoun's own schools. Two of these have good academic reputations and the third, though handicapped by inadequate premises and by the proportion of its pupils who are below average ability, is known for its experimental work with the non-academic child. During the course of this study, for example, this school gained five of the six awards which came to Scotland in the Shankar's International Children's Competition in Art. It was noted as typical of Glasgow schools' staffing problems that, despite the increasing pressures to stay on at school beyond the minimum leaving age, any of its pupils who wished to stay on after 15 had to transfer to another school.

For an area so near to the city centre Dennistoun's facilities for outdoor recreation also appear to be good. Two of the above secondary schools share a large sports field which is literally at their gates. The 104-acre Alexandra Park, hilly and with small areas of woodland and water, provides pleasantly rural walks. It is large enough for a 9-hole golf course as well as for football pitches and tennis courts. Though the area available for scratch football and free play looks ample local people said this was not so. In other parts of Dennistoun, especially towards the south, there is obvious shortage both of official open spaces and of the odd bits of waste ground near home that mean so much to youngsters. Mothers were full of complaints about the lack of places where their smaller boys could kick a ball around without getting into trouble with the neighbours or the police. Swimming facilities at Local Authority baths are easily accessible though not actually in Dennistoun but these baths are old, small and crowded. Dennistoun itself has good private swimming baths but the cost (£4 p.a. for boys of 14-17 plus an entrance fee) made them too expensive for all but a handful of the youngsters of this study.

The local provision for other types of leisure appears to be changing and on the whole declining. There are three cinemas within easy walking distance from the centre of Dennistoun but another three which were actually within the ward have now closed down, one being replaced by a bingo hall. Roller skating has superseded dancing at what has long been one of Glasgow's main dance halls, the Dennistoun Palais. On the other hand the local youngsters have another of the city's largest dance halls within a short bus ride. The more casual type of leisure that centres on pubs and cafes is well provided for locally. There are pubs galore and cafes are numerous, conveniently sited, and open for long hours.

Dennistoun is also fairly well off in social groups for adults. Even if these are not used to any marked extent by adolescents, the odd youngster joins and they step up the level of the local

Fig. 4
Leisure at home, Dennistoun

opportunities for leisure. In or on the fringe of the ward are old-established sports and political clubs, branches of many of the well-known national organisations, eleven co-operating churches in a Protestant Inter-Church Council and two Roman Catholic churches. Organisations for young people's leisure are not lacking and are varied in type. The Local Authority runs recreational clubs and classes in two of the senior schools, many of which are available four nights in the week from autumn to spring. A smaller number have out-door activities in the summer term. The secondary schools, too, provide a variety of out-of-school activities for their own pupils. Units of the voluntary youth organisations, most of them old-established, number about 26.

On the surface Dennistoun would appear to deserve its traditional reputation of being a stable area. The place is changing however. Old-established residents are tending to move farther out of the city and are being replaced by a 'rougher' population. Another indication of change is that many of the local facilities, shops, schools and places of entertainment, are being increasingly used by non-Dennistoun people. The bingo hall referred to earlier is a case in point. Large numbers of its regular patrons come by car and taxi. The tensions to which these changes give rise may well affect the adolescent or indeed he may be tempted to turn them to his own use. Another matter relevant to the local youngsters is that Dennistoun appears to be better provided as regards recreational facilities than is actually the case. The fact that it has not the glaring social deficiencies of the big new housing estates and that overtly delinquent behaviour is not a marked feature of this part of the city may well mask the current needs of Dennistoun's young people. One observant resident was strongly of the opinion that at this stage of flux in Dennistoun's character 'attention paid to the recreational needs of our adolescents might well pay high social dividends'.

Drumchapel, a housing estate on what was open country in 1953, had acquired a population of over 40,000 by 1964. This makes it roughly the size of Perth. Rectangular in shape, it is about a mile and a half by one mile in area. It stands on Glasgow's western boundary and is about 30 minutes' bus ride from the City Chambers. On the other hand it is only 10 minutes' journey to Clydebank, that industrial part of the

Glasgow conurbation with a population of 50,000 which lies on the north-west bank of the river. Thus Clydebank exerts considerable economic and social influence on the new estate. Drumchapel is separated from other large areas of inter and post-war council housing by two barriers, the main road to Loch Lomond and the north-west on one side, and the electric railway to the coast on the other. Eastwards lies the residential burgh of Bearsden. Northwards is unspoiled, upland country. Drumchapel itself, 300 ft. above sea level, is built on two grassy ridges, the 'drums' from which it takes its name. These, and the bumpy terrain between them, make a pleasantly diverse landscape which affords sudden vistas of the Perthshire hills and of the great beaked cranes which mark the course of the Clyde.

Many of Drumchapel's families originally lived in Maryhill, Partick or Anderston. Their former homes in these relatively central areas were probably not so much slums in the accepted sense as housing inadequate by modern standards. Thus, most of the Drumchapel adolescents of this study had probably spent their early childhood under poor physical conditions. Almost the first family met with in this study, one with six children and the husband out of work for a year, had moved into Drumchapel from a room-and-kitchen home. Drumchapel's very standardised housing is chiefly of the traditional Glasgow terrace type, three or four storeys high, the entrance by an open close, and with stone, unbanistered stairs. Front gardens separate the houses from the street and there are large, grassed, communal areas at the rear. Roads are wide, the place is windy and there is an air of spaciousness or, according to the eye of the beholder, bleakness. About two-thirds of the 8,700 homes have three apartments, the remainder being mostly four-apartment houses let at a monthly rent and rates of about £8 8s 0d. There is a pleasant town centre with 40 or so well stocked shops, two banks and a main post office. Nearby is a large well equipped health centre, a small busy public library, the factor's office etc. Though this official heart of the estate is not a natural focal point in the sense that one passes through it on the way to other places, it is lively in the daytime. But it dies after six o'clock and at the week-end except that youngsters to some extent mill around there at all hours. So they do outside the only other shops which, 30 or so in all, are grouped in the four neighbourhood units into which Drumchapel is physically though not very obviously planned.

As is to be expected Drumchapel has a youthful population, so much so that adults barely outnumber those aged under 21. At the date of the study the 15-19 population formed about 16% of the total which was nearly twice the national proportion or that for Glasgow as a whole. In a terrace built for the larger households this may mean that an 8-home close may have as many as 32 children. Any entrance to such a close frequently has a dozen or so children playing about it. The first and abiding impression of Drumchapel is that it has an unusually large proportion of those still at the age when they prefer running to walking. In or out of doors the dominant feature of the local scene is youth, with the vitality, cheerful boisterousness and wear and tear on the environment that this implies.

Since Drumchapel offers practically no opportunities for local employment, its workers are commuters all. Several largish firms are situated on the fringe of the estate but they can draw employees from other residential areas nearby. Transport facilities by bus and electric train are good but regarded as very costly in money and time by people who have previously lived in relatively central areas. Two shillings a day in fares is the least that many people expect to pay. Manual work, but not of a highly paid type, is probably the typical job of the Drumchapel man. This is often in the heavy industry of Clydeside. As far as boys are concerned the scaling down of this type of work is reducing the opportunities for apprenticeship. Not a great deal of factory work is available for girls. This is unfortunate since there is a considerable demand from the many girls who have had a relatively limited education. As regards women's employment, the figures from this study showed that nearly half of this sample of the 15-19s, i.e. of those whose mothers were unlikely to be tied by a pre-school child, had a mother who worked. The fact that little part-time work is available locally probably accounts for the fact that nearly one in five had a mother working full-time. At the date of the study there was little evidence of unemployment or of gross poverty, but neither was there much sign of such indications of relative affluence as car-ownership. Many families complained that life was very expensive on this outlying estate and cost was generally the first reason given for wanting to leave.

Most of the 10,000 children of school age are educated in Drumchapel itself. There are 15 primary schools. Two of them, for physically and mentally handicapped children, also serve other areas. At the date of the study there were two comprehensive secondary schools, each with a roll of about 1,000. The three nursery schools cater for 150 of the 2,500 children under 5. Even their waiting lists are often closed. Drumchapel's children not only have the advantage of modern premises and ample playing fields but they are lucky in that their schools have no great staffing difficulties since the estate is easily accessible from the west of the city where many teachers live. As yet there are no day-time facilities for full or part-time further education though there is the usual variety of vocational evening classes.

Although Drumchapel is now ten years old its provision for leisure is of the limited nature associated with a new housing estate. There is little opportunity for window shopping, one of the important leisure-time fillers. Nor has Drumchapel any pubs. When the estate was being planned the Corporation's regulations prohibiting licensed premises in council housing schemes were still in force, so that Drumchapel has not had the chance to evolve the social life that develops round the local pub. The same applies to cafe life. Apart from one which keeps shop hours, the nearest cafe is an 8d bus-ride away. There is no cinema, no billiard hall and no betting shop though there are runners in plenty. The only regular commercial provision for dancing is twice weekly in small converted premises which of course get overcrowded. Throughout this study the youngsters referred to the brawls (involving the police) that were a regular feature of this one dance hall. Other facilities for dancing in this community with perhaps 7,000 people aged 15-25 are dependent on the odd dance which a voluntary organisation or the new Community Centre may arrange.

Drumchapel has many natural features—streams, hillsides and woodlands—that are fine for children's play and which make it a better place for their leisure than for that of the adult or adolescent. There is, however, plenty of free ground for scratch football. The main official open spaces are a 'unit park' with provision for bowling, putting and tennis. Two small 'ornamental lay-outs' are situated in other parts of the estate. All are still raw and as yet the landscaping is such that they are rather dull affairs. Facilities for outdoor sport other than for the school children are less good than the general air of spaciousness would suggest. The schools themselves have fine playgrounds and it is a great asset that many of these are now open after school hours and during the holidays. The use of their playing fields, however, is pretty well confined to school children. Facilities for swimming, a small indoor pool at one of the schools, have been most inadequate, but a public pool of European standard is being built. With club rooms, cafeteria and car park, the estimated cost is £300,000. This sounds a lot of money but the provision is surely justified, not merely for its amenity value but as a boost to Drumchapel's self-esteem.

The majority of the social organisations connected with leisure are linked with one or other of the eleven Churches or with the Local Authority-provided Community Centre. This most attractive and well-equipped Centre, opened in 1964 and costing what, in view of the work it has already accomplished, was a modest £70,000, is plainly meeting a genuine need. Its adult (4/- a year) individual membership is 2,000 and over 1,000 younger people use it. The Centre has fostered the growth of numerous adult and children's groups. It has one club for adolescents. Drumchapel also has about 45 youth groups associated with voluntary organisations and including a vigorous Y.M.C.A. Most are open, but not confined to adolescents, i.e. they get many younger children. The majority are connected with the churches as indeed is a great deal of the social provision. Numerous Local Authority-run clubs and recreational classes for young people operate at three of the schools. A Youth Centre and games hall which the Authority is building at a cost of £62,000 should be a tremendous boon. All in all the leisure-time facilities through formal groups is probably not so much thinner than in many other parts of the city (which is not to say that these are catered for adequately). But most people, of course, do not spend that much of their leisure in a formal group. They make more use of what, in any old-established area, is provided by commercial enterprise. And here Drumchapel has almost nothing to offer. It not only lacks pubs and cafes, but it has not a single place like a hotel or restaurant where the rituals associated with important stages of family life, a 21st birthday or a wedding, can be celebrated *in* the local community. Nor has it any of the traditional spots such as the little corner shop where people forgather informally and where news and gossip get bandied about.

Drumchapel suffers from many of the well-documented social disabilities which beset any large-scale housing scheme brought rapidly into being to meet pressing housing needs. Before being over-critical, the enormous scale of Glasgow's housing problem must be held in mind. The fact that many of Drumchapel's troubles derive from its abnormal population structure also needs to be emphaissed. In any place so brimming with youth, physical damage is bound to be heavy. It also means that the adult population is not large enough to 'hold' undesirable behaviour. Though the children's health is fine there is some evidence among adults of more than the normal load of neurotic illness. One of Drumchapel's doctors recorded double the number of calls per Drumchapel patient than in his other practice in another working-class area but an old-established one. In Drumchapel unimportant illnesses, matters that would normally be shrugged off, loomed large. Another local disability, the untidiness of parts of the estate, with fences knocked down, paving stones torn up, and streets littered with glass, is a distress to many Drumchapel people. Again this scruffiness is partly due to the excessive proportion of the population which is still at an age to kick along, rattle loose, dig out, throw at, push through and climb up any physical object to hand. The fact that no one owns his home and that the garden is a shared 'front' even when one tenant makes himself responsible, means that he finds it extremely difficult to keep the plot tidy. Many garden lovers get so discouraged that they tend to give up the effort. Drumchapel's squalid looks as well as the extent of actual Trouble are undoubtedly among the reasons why a considerable number of families who have lived there for ten years and should by now be forming its solid core, try to move away. They refer first to the cost and fatigues of travel but they also lay considerable emphasis on the less concrete disabilities. Nevertheless, not all the comment is unfavourable. Numerous families were encountered who were reasonably content. Indeed, one or two people were looking forward to the day when Drumchapel might be trying for burgh status.

The West Lothian town of Armadale, midway between Edinburgh and Glasgow and three miles west of Bathgate, is a deceptive place. Motorists speeding down its mile-long main street flanked with low, grey-slated, houses tend to dismiss as a bit of a place what is, in fact, a sizable town. Roughly a square mile in area, it has a population of 6,000 actually in the burgh and another 2,000 on its fringes making it comparable with such a place as Peebles or Oban. The town stands on a wind-swept slope 600 ft. above sea level and snow lies about for days after it has melted in places a few miles away. Armadale has many indications of being an old industrial community. A score of tall black chimneys from a steelworks flank one end of the town and there is a Miners' Welfare on the main street. Reminders of the traditional industry are the many pigeon doo'cots, the auriculas in front gardens and the occasional evocative street name—'Friendship Row' or 'Unity Terrace'. At any hour of the twenty-four small knots of men forgather at the main crossroads. The adolescents too, adopt this pattern. Groups of them and their bikes are always to be seen at this same spot propped up on pub and cafe window sills. Maybe this particular bit of social life is a continuation of the type of leisure that suits the miner since it takes him into the fresh air and fits the needs of the shift worker in that he can depend on finding company at pretty well any hour.

Armadale proper lies behind the couple of main streets. The red brick houses, mostly built in blocks of four and with a garden back and front, are those of any inter-cum-post-war council estate. Though this extensive new housing tends to be stuck on rather than integrated with the older town, it does not suffer from the physical and social isolation of the typical 'estate'. One interesting feature of Armadale is that although the community itself is long settled, a high proportion of the population have been council tenants for a considerable time. In 1963 as many as three-quarters of the 2,000 families were occupying council houses, nearly half of which had been built before the war. That so large a proportion of the population has had to be rehoused suggests the poor conditions that must have obtained when the parents of today's adolescents were youngsters themselves. Despite the expansion, Armadale is fortunate in that its population structure does not appear to have been disturbed. At the time of the study, for example, the 15-19 population was 8·8% of the total, which is much that for West Lothian as a whole.

Some rough indication of Armadale's industrial structure is

provided in the estimated numbers of insured employees at the Bathgate Exchange which is where Armadale registers. The figures (for June 1961) showed 44% of the men employed in mining and quarrying, with work in the distributive trades as the major employment for women. The town's own local pits are now worked out, the last one closing down in 1965. Other traditional employment is in a steel foundry and at a brick and firestone works. Women's jobs are confined to one small hosiery factory and the local shops. The pattern is altering rapidly in that many people now travel to general industrial work outside the town. A good deal of labour goes to the new firms which the Government has helped to promote in the Bathgate area, the British Motor Corporation and the Telegraph Condenser Company in particular. All this means that management now tends to live out of the town. Younger workers, too, have difficulty in obtaining jobs in Armadale. As many as 49 boys were said to have put in an application for one apprenticeship job with the Armadale Council. The figures for entrance to employment at the Bathgate Juvenile Employment Exchange indicate the main types of work in which the adolescents of the district are engaged. These figures, and the information obtained from the youngsters interviewed, suggested that a fairly high proportion of the boys were in apprenticeships and a fairly low one of the girls in clerical employment. Unemployment was less a reality for these younger workers than an apprehension based on the past experience of their families.

Armadale has two primary and one junior secondary school, the latter having a roll of 270. All are short of accommodation and of playing fields. The majority of the town's children, as was the case with 70% of those interviewed in this study, receive all their full-time education in Armadale. Those in senior secondary education travel to Bathgate where there are three schools with rolls of 550, 900 and 950 respectively. They enjoy modern premises and good facilities for games. Further education, too, mostly has to be undertaken outside Armadale. All this helps to explain the high hopes pinned on the new senior secondary school now being built. An attractive new county library is proving an educational and recreational asset to adults and children but, as usual, it plays relatively little part in the adolescents' leisure.

The town is surrounded by open country which means that rural pursuits are fairly easily available. Open spaces for recreation within Armadale are limited to the 'Thistle's' 2½-acre football pitch and to two other sites, neither of which has provision for organised games. Two additional grounds of 11½ acres are about to be laid out. If imaginatively designed and equipped they will be a boon to the adolescents and also to the smaller fry whose unofficial playing grounds, as in so many places, are continually being gobbled up by all the new building.

For a population as large as 8,000 the commercial provision for leisure is limited, though much more adequate than in the case of Drumchapel. There are plenty of pubs, a greyhound racing stadium (reflecting the miner's interest in whippets), a small cinema, regular bingo sessions, and a betting shop. Armadale has no hall large enough to provide the stylish kind of dance which attracts the older adolescent so that local dancing is limited to the odd record hop or dance at the Miner's Welfare or Scout Hall. These are reputed to be cheap and rowdy and the more sophisticated youngsters steer clear of them. Pub life and that centred on the Welfare is vigorous. The adolescents have evolved a social life of their own at the five cafes and the fish and chip shop. The largest cafe, with accommodation for some 50 people, is open until midnight and for seven days in the week. Mothers with prams and toddlers use it for a mid-morning natter, people come in for a snack at dinner time and a considerable proportion of Armadale's adolescent population appears to flow in and out from four o'clock onwards.

The paragraphs on Armadale news in the weekly *West Lothian Courier* suggests that the town has much the type of social organisations one would expect. They include branches of the British Legion, a Darby and Joan Club, a Pigeon Fanciers' Society, Bowling Clubs and, unexpectedly, a Flute Club. Five churches and the Welfare sponsor a good many of these social groups. The year's highlight is the children's Gala Day, inaugurated in 1902, and its accompanying fair. It is an interesting little sidelight on the persistence of traditions about leisure, and also perhaps on the adolescent's nearness to childhood, that this fair (as is the case with the Shows that turn up in Drumchapel every mid-June) is still held in such esteem.

The Youth Service is represented by one or two Local Authority recreational classes at the secondary school and by about nine youth groups, most of which are associated with a church. They cater for younger children as well as adolescents, do not in general meet more than once a week and have a fairly long summer closure.

It is common knowledge that most adolescents in most places disparage the local facilities for recreation, but the extent to which Armadale boys and girls were prepared to travel for their pleasures suggested the limited nature of the town's own provision. Bathgate, a 7d bus-ride, was their first obvious choice for cinemas, swimming, dancing etc. They went considerably farther afield to neighbouring towns for their dancing. Special late buses played an important part here; so did the skaters' buses in the use which the youngsters made of the ice rink at Falkirk, eight miles away. All told, it seemed that the typical Armadale adolescent expected to travel eight miles or so and that those lacking the cash, or maybe the energy, had to make do with a fairly restricted recreation.

Despite the radical changes which Armadale has seen in recent years the town retains many of the characteristics of an old mining community. A modest, even somewhat muted place externally, it does not wear its ideals and aspirations on its sleeve. On the other hand its physical appearance suggests a strong sense of self-respect. The small children are kept tidy, windows shine, and back as well as front gardens are cultivated. The bus shelters are seldom defaced and the seats and pleasant patches of garden which the council has tucked into odd corners remain trim. For all the quiet face that Armadale presents to the world it may well have a sturdy life of its own below the surface. But the facilities it makes for the leisure of its 550 or so adolescents have definitely not kept pace with the town's growth. Neither in number nor variety are they up to the standards of a younger generation which is better educated, more affluent, more mobile and less inbred than was the case formerly.

Chapter IV

METHODS

Both leisure and adolescence are diffuse and difficult subjects for a sociological study however surface its character. Combine the two and what hope is there of getting at anything beyond the obvious? Leisure is a notoriously imprecise concept, while adolescence is a stage at which most youngsters are reluctant to talk about the personal and shifting reasons which determine how and with whom they spend their free time. One of the girls put it in a nutshell—'I like going out and having fun where people don't know me and I don't like telling people what I do.' Three possible methods of getting young people to provide factual material about their leisure were investigated. A so to speak captive group, the juvenile employees of a firm or the students of a further education college, could be visited regularly in the hope that length of contact would establish confidence between adolescent and adult. Another setting where contact might be maintained over a period would be at some place frequented by large numbers of young people, such as a skating rink or a billiard hall. But both methods cut across geographical areas as far as the youngster's home is concerned and this means diversity in the facilities for leisure easily available to him. An examination of how individuals respond to a more or less common set of facilities might be explored by making prolonged contact based on their homes with the total adolescent population of one small area such as a polling ward. But to confine the study to the adolescents of just one part of each of the three selected areas would make it over-intensive and unlikely to produce findings on which to base policy about the provision for leisure. All the above methods were eventually discarded in favour of the classic one of holding a single interview on a set schedule with a sample of the total 15-19 population of each of the three areas. Details as to how the sample was devised are given in Appendix A.

Method and type of sample having been agreed, three other matters had to be decided on. Should the interview include the adolescent's views, for example on the provision for leisure in his own locality, or should it be confined to the facts on what he actually did with his free time? Secondly, was it possible or desirable to attempt any rough assessment of the quality of his leisure? And thirdly, what people were available for interviewing? It was thought that adults who were genuinely interested in adolescents and could establish rapport quickly would draw out fuller information than is normally elicited in the type of interview undertaken by Market Research staff. The obvious source for the kind of people envisaged was the Youth Service but on the other hand youth workers might be suspect in the youngster's eye as trying to push one particular type of leisure. This could affect his willingness to be interviewed and, more important, it might slant his answers. It was finally agreed to build up a team of voluntary interviewers who, whether or no they had experience of interviewing on a sample survey, would fulfil the following requirements. They must be genuinely interested in adolescents. They must have a professional background which, irrespective of type, would guarantee their reliability in following instructions and their proficiency in making accurate notes. Though familiar with the areas where they would be interviewing, they must neither live nor be employed there. Anyone with the above qualifications would presumably also be competent to advise on the general character of the interview. In fact most of those who were finally selected worked out in numerous small meetings among themselves, and tested in pilot enquiries, the way in which the interview should be conducted. They also decided details of the topics to be explored and the exact wording of the questions. It was hoped that the professional standing of these volunteers and their known concern with young people would offset any lack of experience in the techniques of handling a sample. Some 65 men and women took part in the above preliminary stages and from them a team of 43 was built up who worked on the sample proper (see pp. v-vi).

The interviewers decided that a limited amount of background material about the youngster's family, education, job and spending power was needed as well as information on his leisure. They also came to the conclusion that facts alone should be asked for, not views. The one non-factual question which was eventually included, 'What main provision ... would you like to see in this area?', did not produce much beyond stereotyped replies. How to assess the quality of the youngster's leisure aroused conflicting views among the team. Some were strongly against attempting this, others thought that a competent and concerned adult's view would have its value provided the subjective character of the material was recognised and that it was not used statistically. A compromise was reached. This required the interviewer to place the youngster's total leisure pattern on a five-point continuum ranging from 'unusually satisfactory' to 'unusually unsatisfactory'. The interviewer then elaborated the reasons for his assessment in a brief general comment. Examples read as follows:

Girl (18) packer
> This young girl's one big interest is dancing, and she spends all her evenings out of the home at dancing. Would like to spend more time there, but it is limited by money and facilities. She would like to enter competition dancing later. She is quite happy and is hoping to change her job soon to factory work which will give her more money.

Boy (19) welder
> A rather thin kind of leisure, adult in character (pubs; smoking; pigeons; some dancing; billiards). His father told me when I saw him alone that this boy does not (unlike his younger brother) know what he wants. The father did not think a girl friend might be the answer. A rough sort of chap though pleasant enough. Interesting that he reads books on pigeon racing and has taken up his father's hobby, perhaps as a money-making possibility. He much disliked his first job (7 months) at a chicken factory where his job was killing the birds (with a knife).

Schoolboy (15)
> Seems a highly intelligent lad with unusual initiative. Has developed a keen interest in angling and plays table tennis frequently at a club to which his school was invited. Appears very mature and quickly appreciated purpose and possible outcome of the survey. Verbalised on his special position in that his schoolmates came from all parts of the city, etc. Is probably classifiable as 'Unusually satisfactory' but for the fact that he has so little leisure time.

Where should the interview be held? The youngster's home was the obvious place since he was to be located through his private address. But most of the homes would have only one living-room and most of the interviews would probably have to be held at a time when other members of the family were in. This setting might well influence the youngster's answers nor would it be possible to confine the talk to him. No satisfactory solution was found to either matter but in practice they proved less troublesome than had been envisaged. On the whole the youngsters talked freely, and the additional material from others present often amplified and checked that from the adolescent himself. The team also decided to obtain their answers to the set questions in whatever order proved most suitable. Thus the interview might, on occasion, take the form of a general conversation about leisure, the formal questions being introduced and recorded at strategic points. A whole evening might be spent at one home.

The first small meeting attended by those who volunteered to interview in Dennistoun and Drumchapel was typical of the many subsequent ones. Held at the University, it comprised four men and four women. Three were on the staff of the University Psychology Department, two on that of the Corporation of Glasgow's Education (School Welfare) Department, one was the education and training officer of a large engineering firm, one was a marriage guidance counsellor, and another was a member of the staff of the Glasgow and West of Scotland Association of Youth Clubs. The two main topics discussed were an early draft of the schedule and the methods which should be adopted to obtain the boys' and girls' co-operation. An initial meeting of prospective interviewers for Armadale was held at the town's junior secondary school and with its headmaster in the chair. Those attending, all of whom lived or worked in West Lothian though not of course in Armadale itself, consisted of three men and two women—a health visitor, a youth employment officer, a grammar school art teacher, a young businessman, and a county councillor. This meeting took much the same form as that for Glasgow. At these initial meetings the team had a glimpse of the kind of material they were likely to get from the younger adolescent. This comprised a batch of essays from certain schools in the three areas on how one spent one's leisure on a really enjoyable Saturday. The writers were boys and girls round about 15 who were to leave school shortly.

The team preceded their work with the sample proper by undertaking pilot interviews in districts near to the study areas. These were in that part of Dennistoun which lies south of Duke Street, in a corporation housing estate (Blairdardie) just south of Drumchapel, and in a village (Blackridge) $2\frac{1}{2}$ miles west of Armadale. Pilot and main areas are roughly akin in employ-

On Saturday I get up about 6.45 AM get dressed and put on my heavy clothes, after I get dressed I pack all my fishing gear, 2 rods 2 reels and all my tackle and my gaff or landing net. After my breakfast I then go down to the fishmongers to buy herring to use as bait while pike fishing. I then go by bike to one of many lochs around Milngavie and Strathblane, and proceed to fish till about 6.30 PM in the evening. (Boy)

to the shops. About six o'clock at night I can go out with my girlfriends to the pictures or to a dance. My mother gives me enough money to pay for the bus fares etc. I like mostly to go to the pictures that's if there's good pictures on. I usually go to the pictures with my girlfriend and two boys. When we come out we usually go to the fish and chip shop then we walk home. Phillis usually goes on home with her boyfriend after we come out of the Chip Shop. My friend does not stand very long as she has to catch a bus. I go in about 10.30 (Girl)

On Saturdays I usually just sit in the house and watch the television until about 6 o-clock when I go to a party or dance or if I havent got tickets for any dances I just go to the pictures. (Boy)

FIG. 5. 'A really enjoyable Saturday' as described by three school children aged 14-15 ment, transport and their provision for leisure. The Dennistoun pilot area has poorer and more uniform housing than the rest of the ward. Blairdardie, like Drumchapel, consists of council housing but it is an older place and has a more varied socio-economic character. Blackridge and Armadale are a fairly similar type of community though Blackridge is an (industrial) village whereas Armadale is definitely a small town.

The initial contacts in these pilot areas were made at 12 addresses drawn at random from the electoral register. A member of the team called, in some cases without previous warning, in others after sending a letter. This asked if the household contained anyone aged 15-19 and if so whether he or she would give an interview for a University study on the leisure-time needs of young people. The 12 addresses were found to contain 27 households and 4 adolescents. All 4 of these youngsters gave an interview on what, at this stage, was an early draft of the schedule. Since the two methods of approach seemed equally satisfactory it was decided to continue with them for further pilot interviews. The schedule itself had to be considerably modified.

Another matter tested in the pilot was the best way of establishing which households on a given list of sample addresses contained one or more individuals of the requisite age. This meant that the interviewer had to find out for *every household* whether it had living in it anyone born between April 23, 1944 and April 23, 1949. Since people were often out and since any information which neighbours might supply needed to be checked, this locating often entailed repeated visits at different times of the day, evening and week. Two minor assets here were Glasgow's clear and consistent method of house numbering and the admirable Scottish custom of having one's name on the front door. These pilot interviews continued to test the use of an introductory letter compared with going in blind, and the formal appointment compared with pressing for an interview then and there. The wisdom of using this second approach in preference to an appointment became increasingly evident. An interviewer who was plunged headlong into the life of the family picked up incidental clues as to why the home's adolescent spent his time as he did. The very informal conditions under which an interview might take place were illustrated at one home where, money for the electric light having presumably run out, adult and boy conducted a lengthy conversation by the light of a small fire and against a background of noise from what seemed to be a roomful of children, birds and dogs. The interviews were often interrupted, as when the family's two-year-old sidled up to the interviewer with the engaging information that he was about to pee; or when a mother, at a Saturday morning interview, bore down with a tray and 'Your breakfast's ready missus.' This last was typical of innumerable kindnesses received. Apart from a limited number of households who figuratively and literally slammed the door in the interviewer's face, and a few curmudgeonly parents who refused the interview without ever consulting their youngster, relatively few families were impatient with the study nor did they seem to regard an unannounced visit as an intrusion. Indeed many parents were genuinely pleased that anyone, and particularly someone from the University, should take an interest in their adolescent children. The youngsters themselves gave the impressions that they were rather flattered to be consulted. It made them 'feel somebody'. All told, the number of pilot interviews held, and to which the above comment refers, was a hundred and twenty three.

When the sample itself came to be devised professional advice was taken on the type most suitable. The 15-19 age group is an awkward one to sample statistically since its whereabouts cannot be found from the electoral register nor can current addresses be obtained from education and health authorities as is sometimes possible when sampling a child population. Ministry of Labour records, too, present difficulties. The method finally adopted (Appendix A) was the standard one of listing all the addresses, as given in the electoral register, for the enumeration districts covered by the three areas. A sample was then drawn from these addresses of a size to produce a predetermined number of those aged 15-19. For Dennistoun and Armadale this number was 200 each, and for Drumchapel 400 since the population there much exceeds that of either of the other areas. This list of addresses, together with the surnames of each of the households resident at them (which in tenements often numbered 8 or more) was divided into 20 sets. To save labour each set related as far as possible to neighbouring streets. A typical set, e.g. one of those for Drumchapel, contained 120 or so households.

The interviewing proper got off to a good start on September 1, 1964 with a meeting at the University. Nearly all the team were present together with certain other people who had shown particular interest in the study. This meeting was held partly to emphasise the break between the uncertainties of the methods experimented with at the pilot stage and the clear-cut ones required for the interviewing proper, and partly to stress the importance of the subject to which the team members had committed themselves.

The target date for the interviews to be finished was December 31 and most of the lists were completed on time. Unfinished ones were shared out among the team, the final interview taking place in February. A few further meetings were held to talk over particular points that had emerged in the interviews. The team were also asked to provide brief written answers to questions on their general impressions. Typical extracts read as follows.

> *What kind of leisure activities did the boys and girls you interviewed seem to be frustrated about or to avoid?*
> Most avoided activities which could be broadly described as creative and demanding of self. (Drumchapel)

> *What kind of leisure activities did they enthuse about, or if not enthuse, seem to derive pleasure from?*
> They didn't enthuse about anything. They were keen on the cafe life. (Armadale)

> *How would you define the 'typical Scottish adolescent' you have met in these interviews?*
> Rather confident, prefers being in a crowd, and somewhat lacking in ambition. (Armadale)

Analysis of the address lists showed that there remained 79 'cases' on which the information required was still missing. In most instances the 'cases' were adolescents who had refused the interview or had had it refused for them by someone else in the home. The remaining blanks referred not to an adolescent but to an address at which repeated enquiries had failed to establish whether it contained anyone of the required age. The team came to the conclusion that they had exhausted their own resources as regards the above 79 cases, so the Social Survey and the British Market Research Bureau were asked for professional interviewers. They provided five people (all women) who worked to exactly the same rules as the team except that they were not asked to fill in the final assessment on the quality of the youngster's leisure since these new interviewers had not taken part in the many discussions on this point. The interviewers established which of the above addresses contained adolescents of the required age and they managed to obtain a full interview with all but 33 of the youngsters. Using a new and very short schedule they went back to these 33 'cases' and established certain basic facts (father's job, educational situation etc.) about the background of all but 3 of them. Their results showed that the background of the 30 was much the same as that for the rest of the sample.

By a happy chance the number of boys and girls interviewed on the full schedule, and on whom therefore the tables are based, came to a round 600. Three points to note about the summary given below are that the number of adolescents located was far smaller than that which the sample had been expected to produce; that the refusal rate was gratifyingly low; and that those on whom no information whatever was obtained was only three.

Sample—Number of Adolescents aged 15–19 interviewed (Autumn, Spring, 1964–5)

Area	Adolescents located	Interviewed on full schedule	Refused full schedule	Refused full schedule but interviewed on short schedule	Refused short schedule	No. of adolescents which sample, based on 1961 Census, was expected to produce
Drumchapel	284	272	12	10	2	416
Dennistoun	185	172	13	13	–	222
Armadale	164	156	8	7	1	226
Total	633	600	33	30	3	864

The second part of the study concentrated on obtaining young people's views about their leisure as distinct from the facts which, it will be remembered, was all that the interviews had been concerned with. This next stage was primarily an attempt to find out what his leisure *meant* to the youngster. It was decided not to re-approach the boys and girls of the sample for this new material nor to confine those consulted to the youngsters of the three study areas. Provided the boy or girl lived in the Glasgow area or in the Armadale/Bathgate district, and provided he or she was aged 15-19, any adolescent might be included. A new set of adults, too, was brought in to collect these 'views'. Four men and two women, mostly still in their twenties, undertook the bulk of this work. The chief exception was that some 50 other interested adults held 50 single discussion groups with *ad hoc* sets of adolescents. The groups, quite small and as informal as possible, were organised through firms, stores, churches, schools, colleges, debating and dramatic societies, youth organisations etc. In a few cases the group consisted of a set of adolescents who met at one of their homes. One group only, connected with Drumchapel, became at the youngsters' request a continuous affair. It held 16 meetings, the participants changing to some extent on each occasion. It was interesting that when the study's field work ended this group again asked to be continued and it was taken on for a further year by the University's School of Social Study. This particular group also interested itself in a week's visit to Drumchapel of 21 young workers from Czechoslovakia. The topics most frequently aired in these discussion groups were attitudes to authority, relationships between the sexes, and a host of matters covered by the all-embracing term 'Trouble'. Relatively little cropped up about job, earnings, or public affairs. Views thrashed out related to 'The difference between ladies and girls'; 'Helping with C.N.D. or Oxfam or something'; 'Who ought to pay when a boy takes you out?'; 'Do you need some love before you can enjoy sex?'; and 'Does the colour question matter in Glasgow?' (a topic sparked off by a visit the Prime Minister was making to Rhodesia).

Extracts from notes made by the adult recorder at a couple of the discussion groups read as follows. The first group, associated with a Congregational Church, consisted of 5 girl office workers and a student at a teacher training college.

> The group seemed conscious of difficulties as regards self-government in their own club. They were apparently willing to accept a leader. They gave two examples of reaction to people in authority. 'If you say you are going to be a teacher the boy says Oh Dear and sheers off.' 'If you talk to or of a minister you must keep your face dead straight.'

Another set of notes came from a group connected with a Gorbals Youth Club. The members were two bakehouse girls, a hairdresser's apprentice, a naval cadet and a couple of drivers' mates. Talking about money they said:

> We need it but don't get enough of it. You should watch your money and what you do with it—some folk are dead careless with their money. The

girls thought they were all too careless.... The boys thought they themselves were careful.... One boy—'If I had any more money I would gamble with it—so I don't want any more.' The girls felt that they had to buy more than boys—make-up, clothes etc.—and that it was quite right that the boys should spend money on them.

In all, 76 discussion groups were held, the number of boys and girls consulted in this way being about 600. The great majority were at work, not school.

The second method adopted for getting at views was through written material. This was obtained by asking for sets of youngsters aged 15-19, e.g. a class at a college of further education, to write their answers to questions broadly connected with leisure. Firms, youth groups and a wide variety of educational institutions co-operated. Since the boys and girls might not be willing to give their real views if they thought that anyone they knew would read their comments, the adult responsible, the form master in the case of a school group, was asked to see they did not put their name on their papers and to guarantee to the writers that no one except those at the University who were responsible for the study would see what they wrote. The occasional fallacious or salacious paper received suggests that the youngsters did feel confident that their anonymity would be preserved. Nor were they afraid to give the occasional rap as in the case of the boy who, asked whether he thought cafe-going a waste of time, wrote, 'I think what *you* are doing is a waste of time.'

Examples of their written comment read as follows. The first youngster, a boy of 16 at a senior secondary school, answers a question on how he would advise the Authority in his West Lothian home town to spend £10,000 for the benefit of adolescents.

I would like to see a sports emporium, with facilities for every kind of sport for boys. The girls should have one of their own since they would obviously be a distraction from actual sport. Secondly, I would like to see a new dance hall—with stricter regulations against the standard of entry. Nowadays, you can't go into a dance hall without some one pointing a 'knuckle-duster' or something similar at you. Can't one enjoy a night out with a girl in peace, without this pestering? I want to see a dance hall for the average teenager—not for the candidates for the asylum. Thirdly, although I probably have already exceeded my £10,000 limit, I would be very grateful, and so would we all, for a sort of club-room which would house a membership club only, you know—somewhere where we teenagers could meet to sing, talk with each other and play some quieter games.

The second writer, a 15-year-old boy at a junior secondary school, refers to what he thinks older people do not understand about teenagers.

> Well your parents for a start. Their idea of fashion is rotten, they want you to wear big baggy trousers and big notted ties and big daft shoes which are called beatle crushers and take the police you might be walking along the street and they pull you up a close and If you have a wepon they will kick you head In.

A different type of written material was obtained from just a few adolescents who, contacted by one of the field workers, kept brief diaries for this study. Some of this comment was unusual, as in this extract.

> I often think what is it like to be free from time for we are bound by time even if we stop or throw out all our clocks. . . . Time has elapsed since when I started writing until now as I go on writing or talking. I sometimes stop and stand or sit very still and think what is me and never seem to be able to get a satisfactory answer.

Another diary keeper, a boy of 15, had a more earthy outlook.

> Friday evening I went out in an ice cream van. It was a bad night for me because most of the people were a bit crabit. . . . Near the end of the run my girl friend came out and talked to me, but the driver of the van was impatient because we were running late and he had a long journey home. After about half an hour my girl friend decided that it was getting late so she went away home and so did we. On Saturday morning I had a long lie and when I got up I read my weekly comic and went to help my dad fill up the three vans. . . . I went into the cafe and had a carry on with some girls that were there that I know. Later on my friend came in and we made arrangements for —— pictures where there is plenty of talent. On Saturday evening a last minute decision was made that we should stay at home. It was the first time for quite a while that I had stayed in the house and it was destorbing having to put up with adverts every ten minutes it was the longest Saturday night I had ever spent because I could not sleep during the night.

All told, about 1,600 adolescents provided written material. A limitation of its value was that the bulk came from those still in full-time education which meant that it tended to exclude the opinions of the older adolescent. A final comment on all this 'views' material is that it was impossible to assess its weight. No more should be read into it than that a fair number of boys and girls appeared to think this or that.

An entirely different type of information was obtained through drawings. This type of comment was used on the assumption that the artist has a clearer insight than the ordinary person. Three young and professionally trained artists made studies of the local scene in Dennistoun, Drumchapel and Armadale, while certain younger boys and girls (aged 14 and 15) made their own pictorial comments on leisure.

A fourth source of material were the 40 boys and girls known as the Leavers. Three secondary schools, one in each of the study areas, introduced two members of the team to pupils picked at random from those who had recently had their 15th birthdays and intended to leave school at the end of the term (Easter 1964). The adults kept up the contact for the next two years, chiefly through intermittent visits to the youngster at his home. In most cases it was a casual, surface-level relationship but a fairly close one, fostered on both sides, grew up with a dozen or so of the Leavers and their families. Unfortunately one of the two adults left Glasgow before the two years were up so that a new adult had to be introduced in the case of half the Leavers. With the other half the relationship was uninterrupted and the youngster's family came to regard their team member as someone who was interested in how their son or daughter was getting on in general rather than as someone making a study of how the youngster used his free time. There was little indication that the contact disturbed normal patterns. This particular piece of field work had two main purposes, to

Fig. 6. Motorbike owner

see whether the boy or girl made important changes in the way in which he spent his leisure, and, more important, to try to get to know just a few individuals fairly well. The Leavers and their families certainly helped to give flesh and blood to the material on 'views' and to the facts elicited by the interviews.

CHAPTER V

THE FACTS—AS SHOWN IN INTERVIEWS
WITH A SAMPLE OF THE 15-19 AGE
GROUP IN THREE AREAS

Introduction

This chapter discusses the reactions of the boys and girls of the sample to whatever facilities for leisure were reasonably available to them and it explores some of the reasons that seemed to determine the use they made of the provision. The facilities were classified according the way in which the youngster used them rather than by type. The first category dealt with leisure spent at home. Examples of this were 'Listening to my favourite American rhythm 'n' blues record', or 'My boy friend came in and we watched T.V.' The other three all related to leisure spent outside the home. Leisure I, which covered a wide range of interests, was in the main the more casual and self-run kind of recreation. It tended to be undertaken with just one or two friends, or even alone. The activities listed included such things as scratch football, snooker, golf, swimming, 'Visiting my uncle', fishing, baby minding at someone else's home, and 'Out, but doing nothing in particular'. Leisure II comprised most of the main popular types of recreation which commercial enterprise provides and which the youngster mostly used on an *ad hoc* basis. Those listed were cinema-going, dancing, cafe and pub-going, ice-skating, ten-pin bowling and spectator sport. The final category, leisure spent on an activity provided through some formal group, necessitated membership of an organised society, adult or otherwise. Sports clubs, dramatic societies, folk-song groups, Orange Lodges and all the units of organisations connected with the Youth Service were included in 'Formal Group'.

The tables relating to the sample of 600 adolescents who were interviewed were broken down by sex, age and current educational situation, i.e. whether the youngster was or was not still in full-time education.[1] As regards age, this refers to the boy's

[1] See footnote to List of Tables (p. xii).

TABLE 1

Composition of sample in relation to sex, age and current educational situation

Age	Male							Female							Male and Female					
	15	16	17	18	19	N.I.*	Total	15	16	17	18	19	N.I.*	Total	15	16	17	18	19	N.I.*	Total
In full-time education	22	21	10	5	3	—	61	19	8	12	4	4	1	48	41	29	22	9	7	1	109
Left full-time education	31	47	70	40	43	—	231	32	66	62	44	56	—	260	63	113	132	84	99	—	491
Total	53	68	80	45	46	—	292	51	74	74	48	60	1	308	104	142	154	93	106	1	600

Composition of sample in relation to age groups (%)

	M	F	T
Age group 15–17½	66	63	64
Age group 17½–19	34	37	36

Composition of sample in relation to current educational situation (%)

	M	F	T
In full-time education	21	16	18
Left full-time education	79	84	82

* N.I.—No Information

or girl's age at April 23, 1964. Since the interviewing took place between September 1964 and April 1965 none of those interviewed was under 15½ and some had reached 20. Thus any youngster who was still in full-time education had stayed on voluntarily after the minimum leaving age. The fact that the interviews were held in the autumn and winter also needs to be borne in mind since patterns of leisure are so often seasonal.

TABLE 2

Composition of sample in relation to area and age (%)

	M 15–17½	M 17½–19	F 15–17½	F 17½–19	T 15–17½	T 17½–19
Drumchapel	14	7	16	9	30	16
Dennistoun	10	4	9	5	19	9
Armadale	8	6	7	5	15	11
All Areas	32	17	32	19	64	36

Drumchapel comprised 271 or 45% of the 600 adolescents interviewed (Tables 1, 2). Dennistoun, with 173 and Armadale, with 156 had much the same numbers. The sexes, 292 boys and 308 girls, were about equally divided for the whole sample and also for each of the areas. The largest single age group was that of the 17-year-olds. Those above this age were fewer than those below it, which corresponds with the age structure in Glasgow and in Scotland generally. The fact that a larger proportion of the sample was aged under rather than over 17½, and also that the non-statistical 'views' material came chiefly from this younger set, means that the study tends to relate to the lower half of the 15-19 age group. The great majority of the sample (82%) had, of course, left full-time education. The 'typical' adolescent of this study could be described as a 16½-year-old boy or girl who, leaving school at just 15, had now been out at work for 18 months.

The adolescents' background

A family containing any child as old as 15-19 is, of course, likely to be a completed one. The figures showed the weighted average household size of the sample adolescents to be somewhere between 3 and 6 persons, but a third of the boys and girls had 6 or more persons in their home and 8% had at least 9 (Table 3—Appendix C). Drumchapel had 43% of such households, Dennistoun only 17%. The home with a larger than average number of dependent children tends to be a poorer than average one and if its adolescent member is at the top end he may well have had a thinner childhood as regards material benefits than that of his contemporary with fewer siblings.[2] Size of family and educational attainment are also linked. The large family is less likely than the average sized one to keep a child on at school after 15. This study showed that while 22% of the youngsters in a 2, 3 or 4 person household were still in full-time education, this held for only 12% of those in the larger (7 or more person) household. As will be shown later, educational level was very relevant to the study in that it bore closely on the youngster's use of formal groups. A larger than average household also increased the pressure on space in the youngster's home. A single living-room and no yard or garden had a limiting effect on what he could be expected to do with his free time. In the evening or at the week-end this one living-room practically always had several people in it. Visitors had to be entertained there and, what with family and friends, it was common enough to find seven or eight people present. Congestion was added to by the T.V., and by the fact that any activity in the kitchen, which normally lead off the living-room, was audible. Except in the one or two-child home it was unusual to come across an adolescent who had a bedroom to himself. A case in point and one which excited no comment from the youngster's family, was that of a 17-year-old girl who shared a tiny bedroom with a married sister, the latter's husband, and their year-old baby. Compared with middle-class homes, these working-class ones continually emphasised the difficulties of using leisure for such things as solid reading, dress-making, bike-mending, constructing fragile, bulky and messy objects, or indeed for any pursuit that requires a measure of quiet, space and storage room. On the other hand, in certain ways the youngster in the larger than average family was not necessarily at a disadvantage. Such boys and girls often had a large circle of friends who came in and out of each other's homes and in general made a robust social life among themselves.

[2] 'Family Poverty'. *Case Conference*, Vol. 12 No. 10, April 1966. *The Poor and the Poorest: A New Analysis of the Ministry of Labour's Family Expenditure Surveys of 1953-54 and 1960*. Occasional Papers on Social Administration No. 17. Bell, 1965.

The smaller than average families were also unequally distributed. Whereas Dennistoun had 33% of small homes with 3 or less persons and Armadale 27%, Drumchapel had only 13%. The adolescent in such a family, if not an only child, was probably the only one still at home, with all the material advantages that this implies. The mother could work full-time if she chose to do so while the youngster probably had a bedroom to himself, got a holiday away and had good equipment for hobbies. By and large this smaller home was one where the parents looked ahead and put some pressure on their child to take an apprentice type of job and to keep up evening classes. There was also some evidence that the parents encouraged him to belong to some type of formal group.

One further point about the adolescent's family that bore closely on his life was that more than one in ten had no father and in a further 28 cases the father was an invalid, unemployed etc. (Table 4). An unexpected feature about Dennistoun, as shown in the sample, was that the proportion of boys and girls whose father or mother was dead was considerably higher than in the other two areas. Was this perhaps connected with the age structure of the district, or with the character of its housing? In these homes and in the motherless ones the youngster often needed extra help as regards his leisure. All told there was a good deal of imprecise evidence that family structure exerted considerable influence on the leisure pattern of the children even when they were in their mid and late adolescence.

From what was known of the housing of the three areas it was expected that most of the fathers would be manual workers.[3] Since these fathers were unlikely to have been born later than the end of the 1920's, they were the adolescents of the depression years with all that this implied for their generation as regards entry to the labour market and opportunities for technical training.[4] Thirty-four per cent of the adolescents had a father who was in the skilled manual category, the group IV of Table 4, while 27% had a father in some other type of manual

---

[3] For this study the father's job was not classified by Ministry of Labour groupings but so as to suit the types of work most likely to be found in the three areas. The interviewers probably established groups I, II, III and VII fairly accurately but were less confident that they had distinguished IV from V.

[4] *The Young Wage Earner.* Ferguson and Cunnison. O.U.P., 1951.

work. Dennistoun differed markedly from the other areas in that a much higher proportion of the youngsters had a father in what might be classed as a white-collar job. Analysis of the sample as a whole showed that those with fathers in this latter type of work were kept on at school after the statutory leaving age much more than was the case with those whose fathers were manual workers. The figures were 28% for those with fathers in Groups I, II and III; 19% for Group IV; and 17% for Groups V, VI and VII. The pattern is the expected one but it is referred to here because, as said before, the youngsters still at school or college reacted so differently from those who had finished with full-time education in the use they made of formal groups.

Rather less than half of the boys and girls had a mother who worked, nearly half of these mothers doing so full-time (Table 5). The Armadale mothers were less likely to work than those in Dennistoun or Drumchapel but a larger proportion of those who worked did so full-time, probably because Armadale has few local opportunities for part-time jobs. Rather more of the adolescents who were still in full-time education had a mother who worked than of those who had left school. Was it the mothers' earnings which helped to keep them on at school? The pros and cons of mothers going out to work played little obvious part in this study of children as old as adolescence. The youngsters themselves did not comment on it adversely, domestic chores did not appear to bother them, and they were old enough to realise the benefits of the extra money. Possibly they appreciated having a mum who moved in a wider world than that of the housewife; possibly it made for better relationships between the generations.

This study, of a sample of the 15-19 population in three areas which are believed to have numerous counterparts in Scotland, showed that even today not more than 1 in 6 was still in full-time education (Table 1). Again there were marked differences between the areas. Whereas Dennistoun had 28% still at school or college, Drumchapel and Armadale had only half as many, 15% and 14% respectively. Dennistoun's more varied housing and social structure were presumably relevant issues and another factor may well have been that its two senior secondary schools have a very good reputation. Geographically, too, Dennistoun is well-sited as regards the city's educational facilities. It was interesting that so many of the adolescents of an ex-mining community like Armadale had chosen to stay on at school after 15 even though they had no facilities in the town itself. Another area difference was the the girls in Drumchapel had continued at school only half 'as well' as the boys. In both the other areas the sexes showed no difference. Of those in the whole sample who were still in full-time education, 61% were at a senior secondary school (Table 6). Just 24 individuals were at technical colleges, training colleges or a university, the numbers for boys and girls being about equal. Analysis of the school or college last attended (or being attended currently) showed about 20% of the sample to be at a Roman Catholic institution.

The educational background of those who had left school, based on the school they last attended, showed that 42% had been at a junior secondary school, 35% at a comprehensive one (Table 6). Ninety-two per cent of this sample of the 15-19 age group had left school at 15 and this, it must be remembered, means that they probably left when they were just 15, not when they were nearly 16 (Table 7).

How much further education had these youngsters received? No attempt was made to analyse this in detail since memories are short and, in the case of the older adolescents, they might have to recall things that happened as long as four years past. But the figures could be relied on for those who said they had never been in any kind of educational class since they left school, and also for those who were not currently in any type of further education. Seventy-eight per cent of the boys and girls had had no contact with further education in the past, and 73% were having none currently (Table 8). In this matter of further education the girls were doing less well than the boys, more than four times as many boys as girls currently getting day release or some other type of further education apart from evening classes. Even when these classes (which in the girls' case mostly meant shorthand and typing) were added to other types of further education, only 14% of the girls were involved compared with 47% of the boys. Girls' participation also dropped off markedly with age. Eighteen per cent of the younger girls were currently receiving some kind of further education, only 8% of the older ones. The Drumchapel girls again showed up poorly. Of the 133 who had left school, only

13 were getting any further education, a sobering thought.

The following list, drawn from consecutive schedules in each of the three areas, indicates the kind of jobs in which those of the sample who had left school were employed.[5]

Age/Sex	Nature of Job	Type of Employment
17(b)	Guillotine assistant	Paper mill
17(g)	'Straightens wires to put through machines'	Large industrial concern (light engineering)
16(b)	Apprentice moulder	Steel works
18(g)	Shop assistant	Butcher's shop
19(g)	Plastic moulder	Large industrial concern (light engineering)
18(b)	Clerk	Insurance firm
18(g)	Flat machinist	Small textile works
16(b)	Apprentice painter	Local Authority (Works Department)
15(b)	Copy holder	Printers
16(b)	Errand boy	Grocer's shop
15(g)	Sales assistant (unemployed)	Draper's shop
19(g)	Bookbinder	Printers
17(g)	Comptometer operator	Builders' merchants
16(g)	Not in employment	Housewife, pregnant
16(g)	Not in employment	Housewife with baby
19(g)	Cigar machine stemmer	Large industrial concern (tobacco)
18(g)	Receptionist	Butchers' outfitters
18(g)	Clerkess	Meat Market offices
18(g)	Receptionist and clerical worker	Architect's office
17(g)	Junior clerkess	Butchers' outfitters
19(b)	Apprentice electrician	Local Authority (Housing and Works Department)
16(g)	Wages clerkess	Hosiery works
15(g)	Office junior	Brewery office

It was difficult to assess the level of the youngster's job merely from what he had to say about it himself and the classifications in Table 9 are probably imprecise except in the case of apprenticeship and training for a profession. It was encouraging to find that over half of the boys were in this group. On the other hand more than a third were in the 'Other' category which probably represented the unskilled job, dull, and with few prospects. Examples were the boy who prepacked coal, the rope worker who said he did 'anything' and

[5] For a valuable account of adolescents and their first years at work see *Into Work*. Carter. Pelican, 1966.

the van boys (to be seen in Fig. 7). It was particularly hard to establish the level of the girl clerical worker. She might be anything from a junior filing clerkess to the manager's personal secretary. But even when all the girl clerical workers, irrespective of their job level, were added to the tiny number of girls in the apprentice group, well over half remained in the low level 'Other' type of job. This 'Other' group included a tail-end of a dozen individuals who did not reckon to work. The boy had some physical or mental handicap, or the girl was pregnant, or had a baby. Even at this age one or two were in charge of a motherless home. Little of the existing provision for leisure fitted the very special needs of these non-workers.

Another aspect of the youngster's experience of work was the number of jobs he had held (Table 10). As many as 61% of the boys and 50% of the girls were still in the job in which they had started and even of those as old as 18 and 19 nearly half had one job only. Twenty-nine per cent had only held two jobs. Bearing in mind that this figure includes the youngster who had recently started work, it certainly does not suggest overmuch movement. In any case, some change of job in the first

FIG. 7. Boys, aged 16-17, unloading a lorry

few years of work may be an educational experience. It is the constant chopping and changing which suggests a disturbed adolescence. A final comment concerns those who were officially unemployed on the date they were interviewed. There were only 15 such youngsters so that, happily, unemployment was not distorting the general pattern of the leisure of these 600 adolescents of the mid 1960's.

The popular image of today's adolescent as having money to burn was certainly not true of the great majority of these Scottish boys and girls. Overtime and bonuses stepped up earnings but their take-home pay was under £5 for 41%, and only 7% were in the £9 or over group (Table 11).[6] Though earnings rose with age (the wages of a well-paid girl factory worker might increase from 65/- to 144/6 in four years), nevertheless 41% of those aged 17½ and over were only in the £5 to under £7 range. Information about the take-home pay of a few of the girl Leavers during their first two years of work showed that this only rose from the £3-£4 to the £4-£5 group. Earnings were more uniform in the younger than in the older age groups but there were many inconsistencies in both. Opportunity as well as ability was, of course, a key factor. Smoking habits were thought to throw some light on income (Table 13). All three areas showed the ratio of those who spent anything on cigarettes as 1 to 2 for the boys and about 1 to 3 for the girls. The 'average' boy smoker spent under £1, the girl under 10/- a week on cigarettes. What they had to say about their savings indicated that few envisaged being able to afford such big buys as a motorbike or a holiday abroad. Very few of the boys of the sample possessed a motorbike, though in Drumchapel the number of motorised boys grew visibly and audibly during the course of the study. Nor did their homes give much impression of affluence. The parents did not appear to make their adolescent children the elaborate presents which eke out relatively low earnings.

Not earnings but spending money was the relevant issue for this study. Though family patterns of how income is handled vary enormously it was generally agreed that up to about 18 you give your wage packet to your mother who provides necessities and pocket money, 'necessities' being defined in

[6] Figures relate to those in full-time work. They do not include, for example, earnings from a paper round.

innumerable ways. What you earned rather than your age was often the deciding factor as to when you 'went on your own can'. Board money was said to be about £3 for a boy, £2 for a girl. It was normal for those in full-time work to keep any overtime and bonus money, but schoolchildren who had part-time jobs were expected to hand over some of their pay. For example, a schoolboy with a 25/- weekly paper round was giving his mother 10/-, saving 7/6 and keeping 7/6. Pocket money was not high. In the younger age group 59% said, of last week's spending money, that it was under £1 (Table 12). In the older age group 55% said it was £1 to under £3, but relatively few appeared to be at the top end of this range. The typical sum for those under about 18 was probably £1 to 30/-. Three girls on whose information the writer could rely were only having £1 pocket money even at (just) 17 and they did not seem to get much in the way of perks from parents or older siblings. The girls in general had lower pocket money than the boys but, as they pointed out, boy friends helped them out as regards the costs of their leisure.

The youngsters gave the impression of being not all that concerned with money. They were oddly vague as to what, in fact, they earned and the what and when of their next rise. Nor did they complain about home not giving them higher spending money. They had less obvious drive as regards money than was noted among adolescents known to the writer in various working-class districts of London. Parents, too, seemed rather less conscious than their London counterparts of the obligation to give their children what they themselves had lacked—'we had to do without so much'.

The last general point examined was how much time the youngsters had which they could call their own. Most of those at work seemed to be out of the house by 7.30 a.m. and back by 6.00 p.m. A limited number, those with long journeys, evening classes or overtime, had a very much harder day. One record which was probably typical was that of a 19-year-old clerkess on a 5-day-week who left home at 8.15 a.m. and was back by 5.30 p.m. In her previous job as a comptometer operator she had been away from home from 8.45 a.m. to 6.15 p.m. and had also worked on alternate Saturdays, which meant she got back at 1.15 p.m. A rough analysis of the *potèntial* free time in the life of an actual youngster (chosen almost at random) suggested that the number of hours in the year which he could really call his own was about 3,000[7] Since a long week-end offers valuable opportunities as regards leisure, the extent to which the youngsters had the whole of Saturday free was also looked into. Only about half the sample (i.e. including those at school) had the whole of Saturday free. This figure included those who voluntarily took on Saturday work. Those still in full-time education were more likely to keep their Saturday free than those at work. Rather more of the boys than of the girls at work and rather more of the older than the younger age group had a free Saturday. Perhaps the younger ones needed the money more badly, or maybe going out to work was still novel enough to have its attractions. Overtime was more frequent than had been expected considering that two in three of those at work were under 18. All told, the amount of leisure available to the youngsters outside their normal working day was considerably depleted by the additional work which they elected to take on. In view of what was seen of their general attitudes to money would they have cut down this extra work had their opportunities for leisure been more stimulating? It is doubtful whether at this stage of their life overtime was in their real interest.

Leisure spent at home

The youngster was asked what sort of leisure-time activities he was keen on and about how often in the week he reckoned to do something about them. A useful additional question was 'How did you spend yesterday evening?' The interviews themselves, the many hours spent in the Leavers' homes, and the innumerable casual contacts made in the three areas, showed how often their leisure did not, in fact, fall into the neat compartments which the statistical material of this study rather suggests. Moreover a great deal of their leisure was not spent on any definite activity and even when one particular interest was named it frequently overlapped with another. The following diary is a warning that any figures connected with

[7] The boy, a clerk of 17, worked from 8.00 a.m. to 4.00 p.m. on a 5-day week and did little overtime. He had 2 weeks annual holiday, 2 days each at Christmas and New Year, and 1 in September. Thus, deducting his travelling time of 1½ hours a day and allowing 8 hours for sleep he had about 63 free hours in a week, or 3,100 of the 8,760 hours in a year.

a particular activity and the extent to which it was pursued probably gives a more cut and dried picture than was the reality.

Thursday, October 7, 1965. Came home from work about 5.30 p.m. and had my tea about 6.15 p.m. Afterwards I sat down and read the paper, and watched some of the T.V. Later on went out to the local cafe and had some conversation about POP MUSIC, SPORT, and what we would do at the weekend. Left cafe about 10.30 p.m. and came down the road, had a smoke at the corner of the street, until our eyes were getting rather tired so we went up the road to our homes. Sat down in room and wrote this note, and some supper then went to bed about 11.45 p.m.

Friday. Started my evening out about 8.00 p.m. after watching television of an hour and a half. Went down to the billiard hall and had a couple of good games of snooker (I got beat), then left again about 9.30 and went over to the pub, for a couple of pints of lager. Then about ten past ten I was thrown out as it was after time. From there I went up to the cafe to see the mates, who had gone to the dogs at Shawfield, I would have been there also but hadn't the time. We then left the cafe about 11 p.m. After a good night out, I went to bed about 12.30 a.m.

Another diary shows how difficult it was to pin down how leisure is likely to be used.

I arrived home. I lit the fire and made myself a cup of coffee. I wonder what I will do tonight? Yvonne, my friend, is going to night school, so I can't go out with her. If Jean Marc was here I would be going out with him, but he is in France. Maybe I will just watch television or help Mum put up the new curtains. If only the baths or the cinema were nearer. Still it might come one day, but maybe I will be too old to enjoy it then.

The adolescents, and in particular the girls, spent a very considerable amount of their time at home, or if not actually inside the house, in casual contact with it. A question in the interview on what the youngster had done on the previous evening showed that, dismissing the 17 who were at educational classes or who gave no information, rather more had been at home than out on a Tuesday and a Thursday and only slightly less had been in than out on a Monday and Sunday (Table 14).[8] It must be remembered that nearly half the boys and girls were in the unskilled, 'Other' type of work, i.e. a job that might be physically tiring. Also many of them were still growing rapidly. One of the obvious features about the Leavers was how rapidly they shot up during the two years' contact. Another induce-

---

[8] cf. the figures for three or more evenings spent at home in week prior to interview—Grammar and technical school boys 46%, girls 58%; modern and all age school boys 34·6%, girls 62%. *15 to 18 Report of the Central Advisory Council for Education—England*. Vol. II.

ment to spend the evening at home that operated in Drumchapel and Armadale was that many had a long journey to work. Any Drumchapel home-going bus is likely to contain a youngster who is nodding off. Nor was it so unusual, on a chance evening visit, to be told that the boy was asleep, or indeed to find him so, sprawled before the living-room fire. Time, cost and fatigue were powerful inducements to stay at home, especially in bad weather.

A good many of the youngsters gave the impression that almost the only answer on how to spend one's time when at home was to watch the telly. It was practically always on and in a one living-room home can hardly be disregarded.[9] The following run-through of 15 consecutive schedules illustrates the preferences of a few individuals.

T.V. Type of programme preferred	Age, sex and work situation of the boy or girl	
Films, plays, pop	16(g)	Sen. sec. school
Light Programme, Juke Box Jury, Top of the Pops	15(b)	Sen. sec. school
Films and pop programmes	15(g)	Learner button dyer
Detectives, thrillers, pop	16(b)	Postman
Pop programmes	18(g)	Showroom assistant
Sport	17(b)	Apprentice millwright
Serials, detectives, plays	18(g)	Draper's shop assistant
Emergency Ward 10, Coronation Street, pop, Bonanza, Rawhide, Detectives	16(b)	Sen. sec. school
News and serials	19(g)	Shorthand typist
'Anything that's on'	16(b)	Apprentice joiner
Pop music, American films	15(b)	Apprentice fitter
Detective films, pop music	18(b)	Apprentice joiner
Sport, pop music, detective films	15(b)	Pre-apprentice turner
Comedy, political programmes, plays	17(g)	Shorthand typist
Pop	18(g)	Shorthand typist

Pop, well at the top of the list, followed by sport and serials, were the most popular types of programme. The widespread interest in serials suggests less sophisticated tastes than might be expected of this age group. Pop in any form was an almost universal interest. Differences in education and in social background appeared to have little effect on its appeal though there

[9] Week-day viewing figures for all adults (over 15 years) showed that from 6.00 pm.. to midnight those for 'just viewing or listening' far exceeded 'miscellaneous activities'. *The People's Activities*. B.B.C. Publications, 1965.

were indications that the enthusiasm waned in the older age group. Although its pursuit was so widespread there was not much sign that the youngsters followed pop at any depth. Their knowledge was up to date but superficial compared, for example, with the amount of information that the boy football fan often possesses. In this connection, too, it is worth recalling that the daily press, which meets as well as creates demand, devotes much less space to pop than it does to football though, of course, it has a wide age range of readers. The fact that the interest in pop is so general and that it has survived the years so well suggests that it makes some deep-seated appeal without which no amount of commercial manipulation would be effective. The interviewers noted how, after they had asked about things like reading, hobbies and sport, the word 'pop' brought a sigh of relief—'Here's something we *want* to talk about.' They also noted that very many of these homes possessed at least one of the necessary tools—transistor, tape recorder, record player, beat group instrument, etc. Pop also scores over most other interests in that it gets fed cheaply and regularly by T.V., the press, and sheaves of magazines like *Melodymaker* and *Pop Weekly*. Magazines of this type headed the reading matter which the youngster bought, as distinct from what they saw. They even ousted the women's magazines.

One of the interviewers who was a professional musician made the following observations. He pointed out that pop is very much the youngster's own affair, helps to draw attention to his own generation, and is a handy means of annoying adults—'*They* don't like it.' The apt, imaginative names which adolescents devise for groups of their own making, pop and gang alike, contrast with the lack of lively names and nicknames in more formal groups. Pop is also a highly contemporary interest. Its noise and speed, comparable in kind to that of jet plane or hovercraft, smacks of tomorrow. Then too, the din and the darkness of the typical pop scene permit anonymity. You can express your feelings without being observed. Perhaps it even gives a kind of relaxation. The youngster can also identify with the singer: he too is young and misunderstood. Another asset of pop is that it is simple. The words are largely one-syllable, the music repetitive, the beat insistent and the imagery standardised. Anyone can understand it. There are also social and economic assets. A beat group offers the possibility of a meteoric rise to fame. Even though the youngsters are well aware that this is only for the few, there is just the chance. Apart from any hope of real fame and however unknown one's group, it is still something, at 16, to be able to hold a roomful of people. A well known group in one's neighbourhood definitely adds to the standing of the local youngster. Each of the three areas had such a group—'Lulu and the Luvvers' in Dennistoun, 'The Pods' in Drumchapel, and 'The Golden Crusaders' in the Bathgate/Armadale district. The number of groups which make the grade is, of course, infinitesimal. Apart from lack of technical skill, few are sufficiently in the know to get started on the promotion line that leads to the top. Nor does interest in pop seem to develop a taste for rather more sophisticated types of music, for example, that of the folk world. According to one analysis pop is no more than a bastard form of music which 'lessens the pain of youth without any real development'.[10] On the other hand, and for all its limitations, pop has a certain link with the ancient and honourable tradition of minstrelsy. Music and poetry, however debased, are its concern. The comparison is not that inept when one comes across a boy sitting absorbed with his guitar on the steps of his close, or notes the concentration of a couple of brothers and their mates practising in a tiny bedroom for hours on end.

Reading—newspapers, magazines and books—was another of the home interests examined. As many as 82% said they read (or flipped through?) a daily paper (Table 16). Rather more boys than girls did so, probably because of their interest in sport. These newspapers did not range much beyond the *Daily Record*, *Daily Express* and *Citizen*, and the topics looked out for were chiefly sport, pop, crime and the sexy bits. The discussion groups showed that the youngsters derived a lot of their information about the adult world from newspapers and also that they were refreshingly cynical about some of what they read. As regards magazines, 70% read at least one regularly and over a third said they bought at least one themselves. The girls were more intensive magazine readers than the boys, probably because the women's magazines are so numerous. The girls read more of this basically feminine and home-making

[10] 'What do they get from Rock 'n' Roll?' Larner, *The Atlantic*. August 1964.

material than they did of pop and romance magazines combined. It was the younger girls who were the avid story readers, doubtless finding that the tales reflected their own hopes, fears and ideals. Pop headed the magazines read by the boys but they also read semi-technical magazines such as *Buses Illustrated*. Book, as distinct from magazine reading, showed the expected association with educational level. Most of those still in full-time education read books, less than half of those who had left (Table 18). Public libraries were their main source of books but only about a quarter of the sample used them. Information kindly supplied by the public libraries in Dennistoun and Drumchapel indicated a similar pattern since they had relatively few ticket holders in the 15-19 age group. A voluntary helper who did some interesting work on the reading habits of the adolescents in two of the three areas, and who also examined the material obtained from the interviews in the pilot study, obtained much the same picture as that derived from the sample itself. No attempt was made to analyse the level of the youngsters' reading but it gave the overall impression of being fairly ephemeral. Perhaps at this age and for those who have left school at 15 the important issue is less *what* they read than that they should look on reading as one of the enjoyable ways of using leisure.

Apart from pop, and to a lesser extent reading, it was difficult to establish any major interests that the youngsters pursued at home. Girls, in so far as they did anything definite, seemed to concentrate on their personal appearance (ear piercing, hair colouring, etc.), on knitting and, to a much lesser extent, on sewing. If the girl's mother was a 'maker' the daughter tended to follow her example. The boys had a wider range of interests they pursued at home. These included motor-bike and car maintenance, model making, woodwork, stamp collecting, pigeon breeding, a little 'art', etc.

Another aspect of the boys and girls' leisure was how they had spent their summer (1964) holidays. The case for including holidays in leisure spent at home was that although over half of the sample went away for a holiday in 1964 it was mostly a one week affair. (Table 15). Oddly enough the older age group, those of 18 and 19, had been away little more than the younger ones. If the holiday was not a family concern or spent at a relative's home the youngster probably went to some popular resort like Blackpool or Ayr with two or three friends or relations. Thirty-one of the 600 got abroad. Those who did not go away did little out of the ordinary with their summer or indeed with any of their main holidays. A Leaver, for example, 'just stayed in bed till mid-day' for her Easter holiday and one of the boys said gloomily that he would only be bored if he did get a longer break in the summer. It seemed to be less a matter of cost than of paucity of ideas as to how to use a sustained spell of leisure. There is everything to be said not only for encouraging adventurous holidays but merely for the youngster to get away from home and his workaday life. Those in noisy, hustling jobs would have benefited from a seaside or country holiday after the press and pace of the rest of their year. And those of the Armadale boys and girls who were born in the town, had been to school there, and were now employed in the same small community, badly needed the eye opener of a different environment. The rewarding effects of a holiday away were self-evident. It woke the youngster up, made him more vocal and might even bounce him into new activities.

This section on home-based leisure may perhaps fittingly close with a couple of extracts from the brief records that certain of the boys and girls kept for this study. The first, for a Sunday in October, 1965 is from a girl of 17, a shop assistant.

Today I was not at work so I got up about 11 o'clock. After I had my dinner I went into town with my brother-in-law and my niece. We just looked about the shops and then we went and had our tea. As my brother-in-law had to start work at 4 o'clock, I came home on the bus myself with B—. When we got into the house one of our neighbours was in with my mother. After she went away about 5.30 p.m. my mother had to get ready to go to the hospital to visit my brother. We walked down Duke St. as I was taking B— in her pram to meet her Mum. After my mother left us J— and I went into Galls to get wool and then we came home and had our tea. After we had our tea my mum and my brother's friend E— came in. I just sat and watched television and then went to bed about 11 o'clock. E— stayed the night as he was going to collect K— at the hospital as he was being discharged.

The next diary, again for a Sunday, is from an apprentice joiner of 19.

I rose at 10.30 and lazed around until 12.00. I was then forced out into the storm (with the dog). I shambled about for an hour enjoying the Sunday tranquillity, which would have me cheered up considerably by dinner which was not to be served until 2.30. I went home at 2.00 to attend the carving the joint at 2.30, or if you will dinner. After dinner I did the dishes which kept me busy until four when I vanished into my room and read until 6.00 when I smelt the tea a-cooking. I devoured my tea and vanished back into my room and read some. I left the house at 8.00, collected my girl friend, took her to a coffee bar where we chatted for 30 minutes, argued for 40 and made up for 10. This happened because I told her I was going away for the week-end. I took her home at 10.30 and myself at 11.00. Walked the dog and vanished to bed at 11.30.

Leisure I (Casual leisure other than that spent at home)

Almost the only common element in the mixed bag of activities include in Leisure I was that it took place outside the youngster's home (Table 19). Leisure of this type mostly involved just a couple of close friends or a small set who normally spent much of their free time together. The 'Out, but nothing in particular' category might be 'Three nights a week walking around with my friend' for a 15-year-old schoolboy, or 'Sunday night in the chip shop, etc.' for a boy of 17. The activities referred to under Leisure I were often hatched up on the spur of the moment to fill in a blank evening at low cost. Apart from sport, this kind of leisure probably ranked rather low on the youngsters' pleasure scale. It is important to note that, except for scratch football, the questions in the interview from which the tables on Leisure I are drawn did not list any of the activities by name. They merely came out in the youngster's reply as to what *other* things he did besides those which had already been discussed. This particular set of questions came at the end of a long and tiring section of the interview and the material, though accurate as far as it went, may well have been incomplete. Another point to bear in mind is that the figures did not include a sport if it was pursued through a youth organisation. Thus the boy who played in a Scout football team was recorded as a member of a formal group, not as a footballer. This means that the figures in Leisure I understate participation in certain forms of sport. The most interesting point about Table 19 is that so large a proportion of the boys and girls (45%) did not pursue any of the Leisure I interests.

The activities most often referred to were scratch (street) football for the boys and visiting for the girls. Their popularity was confirmed in Table 20 which showed that 21% of the boys had played scratch football in the last seven days and 27% of the girls had been visiting. Scratch football has many assets. It is genuine play, the most indifferent performer can take part, it gets the youngster into the open air, enables him to let off steam and provides some outlet for aggression. There is a sound case for preserving free ground for this type of leisure, especially in crowded areas like parts of Dennistoun or in a rapidly growing place such as Armadale. Otherwise scratch football in unsuitable places will become an even more frequent source of friction than it is already. The police cannot ignore the annoyance caused, while the boys feel it unjust to be booked for what is no premeditated offence but in their own eyes merely a bit of inconvenience to some old codger.

Another of the activities included in Leisure I was swimming. The number of boys and girls in this 15-19 age group who reckoned to go swimming was surprisingly low. Even though swimming was included in the figures for 'Golf and other sports' the total was only 11% (Table 19). The figure may have been influenced by the fact that swimming was not asked about specifically: it merely came out in the youngster's answers to the question on what other things he did. On the other hand neither Drumchapel nor Armadale has local baths and there was bitter complaint about the cost of bus fares in connection with swimming. Dennistoun also complained that the public baths, though near at hand, were old fashioned, packed out and cold. Non-swimmers in general and girls in particular were put off by poor conditions. The case for swimming is self-evident especially when climatic conditions hinder many of the outdoor sports. Apart from its health and life-saving aspects, swimming is one of the few physical activities that can be enjoyed throughout life. It also suits the needs of the increasing numbers who get their leisure at unusual hours and thus may have to spend a good deal of it alone.

The girls took little interest in sport. Area differences, perhaps reflecting educational ones, were worth noting. In 'Swimming, Golf and other sports' for example, only 9 of Drumchapel's 146 girls participated compared with 12 of Dennistoun's 86 girls. General observation of the girls in all three areas suggested that it was a pity more of them had not learnt to enjoy sport. In the first place their jobs kept them indoors and at sedentary work more often than was the case with the boys and they had no parallel physical activity to the boys' scratch football. Secondly they lacked the jolly social life which sport so often fosters. Unlike the boys, the girls made hardly any reference to lack of local opportunities for sport.

The girls' 'visiting' seemed to be mostly a matter of going to the home of another girl or of a boy friend, not of dropping in on relations. This visiting had several assets, perhaps the most important being that it afforded a link between the girl's parents and those key people, her friends. But it also extended the range of places where she could talk about things essential. The girls in the discussion groups made much of their need for a confidant, someone with whom to swop hopes, fears and emotional support. Many homes are too full for private talk of this kind and the cafe, with its competitive atmosphere, is unsuitable. Nor does the normal youth organisation help here since leaders tend to dismiss talk as so much gossip. Few organisations make any actual provision for it.

Leisure I also included various activities connected with the countryside. The boys and girls appeared to do relatively little hiking, cycling, youth hostelling, canoeing, sailing, climbing, camping, etc. Most of those who did were among the minority who belonged to a youth organisation. A few of the Armadale boys got a little rabbiting and fishing. Adolescence is probably not an age at which any widespread interest in natural history is to be expected. But here is a world which might fit the tastes of those who enjoyed Biology at school, or of a boy who sheered off sport but made himself responsible for the front garden, or of a girl who 'really loved flowers'. The point is referred to later (p. 114).

Another activity looked out for in Leisure I was any form of good works—Service—that the youngster might be undertaking regularly. Twenty-six individuals referred to babysitting though this might of course have been primarily a money-making affair. The kind of native, unselfconscious Service familiar to these boys and girls was a face-to-face affair within the family circle or confined to particular friends. A boy would help a younger brother with his homework, or sleep at a widowed aunt's to keep her company. Bringing back generous presents after a holiday, or financing a friend at the week-end were typical of the Service that dozens of the youngsters undoubtedly gave but which did not show up statistically. Service in the current sense of the word was certainly not an obvious feature among the Leavers nor did it attract any serious attention when talked about in the Drumchapel discussion group. The girls were more responsive to the idea than the boys and those who belonged to a formal group were more likely to get involved in Service than the non-joiners.

Fig. 8. Service?

Leisure II (Cinema, dancing, cafe, etc.)

The national figures obtained in the war-time measure of Youth Registration (1942) showed the cinema and dancing as the chief leisure-time activities of the 'unattached' adolescent[11] and in this small study of the mid 1960's the same two things headed the seven commercially provided types of leisure listed under Leisure II. What the youngsters had actually done in the last seven days confirmed the popularity of the Leisure II interests compared with those referred to under Leisure I. During these seven days the 600 sample boys and girls had made at the very least 900 attendances at Leisure II activities. Even this must have been an understatement since the number of those who reckoned to take part in a Leisure II activity twice or more times a week was very considerably larger than in the case of Leisure I. The real enthusiasts, the three or more times a week people, were boys rather than girls. As regards popularity, cinema, dancing, and cafe was the order, 82% referring to the cinema as one of their regular activities, 69% to dancing and 51% to cafe-going (Table 22). The pattern was not markedly affected by either sex, age or educational situation. In the record for the last seven days cinema again topped the list, followed by cafe and dancing for the boys, dancing and cafe for the girls. Forty-four per cent of the boys had been to a cafe at least once, 33% of the girls (Table 23). One area difference which was expected was that in Drumchapel, which has no commercial cafe open at night or on Sundays, the figures were much less than for the other areas.

In view of the spectacular decline in cinema-going in Britain, from an estimated 13 million to $3\frac{1}{4}$ between 1951-65, it was unexpected that the adolescents should go to the cinema so much. On the other hand their age group is much that of the 16-20s, the most intensive of all cinema-goers.[12] Thirty-eight per cent of the youngsters said they went once a week, 16% twice or more times. The cinema has many practical assets as a leisure-time activity. It is open for long hours, thus meeting the needs of those whose leisure occurs at unusual times. It offers the pleasures of choice since most people have relatively easy access to more than one cinema and programmes

---

[11] *Youth Registration in 1942.* Scottish Education Department. H.M.S.O.
[12] *Cinema Advertising in the U.K.* Pearl and Dean Ltd.

PLATE II

Female coal-bearers in Scotland in the 1840s.

Photograph; by courtesy of Trustees, British Museum.

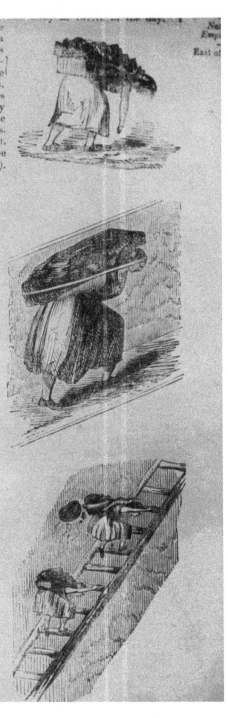

PLATE III

Cafe life, Armadale

Plate IV. Dennistoun

PLATE V. Drumchapel

PLATE VI. Some of the girls, Drumchapel

PLATE VII

At the bus stop, Armadale

PLATE VIII

Close-up, Drumchapel

PLATE IX. Armadale

change every few days. Warm, dark, private, and undemanding as regards conversation, it is used extensively for all stages of courting. There is an old crack that plenty of youngsters would go to the pictures even if no film was shown. Couples at the saving-up-for-marriage stage also opt for the cinema as cheaper than most other popular types of recreation.

The interest in dancing, though common to both the older and the younger group, was rather more pronounced among the girls especially with those at work. Of all the girls, 40% had been dancing in the last seven days (Table 23). Whereas a group of boy apprentices commented that dancing was 'just like standing around at a football match', or 'something you do to pass the night', or 'the only place open after you come out of the pub', for the girls dancing could be an all-absorbing interest. One case in point was a 16-year-old shop assistant who, having already induced an older sister to supplement her pocket money (under £1 a week) so as to step up the number of nights she could afford to go dancing, was now thinking of changing to a factory job for the same purpose.

A group of quite young adults who commented on dancing as one of the youngster's main leisure-time pursuits pointed out that considerable changes had taken place even since they were adolescents. Today's dancing requires less skill than formerly. The semi-darkness in which many dances are held affords cover for the unproficient and so does the music's blare. As with the cinema—'It's nice not to have to talk.' Dances are rowdier, rather less frequented for the sake of the dancing itself or even as an opportunity for meeting the opposite sex than as a chance for a carry-on. The youngsters themselves strongly associated dancing with Trouble—an odd connection one would have thought. Even the dances at church and Scout halls were not immune from fights, and commercially-run affairs, especially at the smaller places, seemed to breed them. Management kept a tighter control over the big popular halls. Pretty well all agreed that the Trouble at dances was associated with drinking. It was notoriously difficult to stop people bringing drink into a dance. The bottle-littered ladies' cloakrooms, as seen at one of the big Glasgow halls chiefly patronised by adolescents, suggests that it is not only the boys who are involved. It was also noted how the character of a dance changed after pub closing time. Up till then girls predominated and danced together but once the hall filled up rows were liable to erupt both inside and on the street.

One problem connected with dancing and younger adolescents is the dance that goes on until the early hours. On Fridays, *the* night for dancing, the popular Glasgow halls close down at one o'clock but the small clubs often keep open until three a.m. At this time of night the crowds hanging round the entrance to the dance and the Friday night drunks and reckless car drivers make a not too desirable environment for 15 and 16-year-olds. But the real problem, and this involves the older adolescent too, is connected with the business of getting home, especially since most of these adolescent dancers do not move in car-owning circles. Those from Drumchapel either get the last and therefore crowded and rowdy service bus at 11.30 p.m., which means leaving the dance early, or they have to wait about for the special, once an hour buses that operate up to three o'clock, after which the service ceases until six o'clock. Their answer is to share a taxi, or to scrounge a lift, or to beg a bed at the home of a friend of a friend (with the risks implicit in these hastily contrived arrangements). Most wait for the hourly bus which, on wet and wintry nights, is not much fun after the hot dance hall and for people wearing thin clothes and shoes. Armadale too, has plenty of late-night dancing which involves travel but in this case special dancers' buses are often available. Yet another problem connected with late-night dancing as a *regular* feature is that in the case of the younger girls it is a constant source of friction between parent and adolescent.

Cafe-going played a key part in the youngsters' leisure particularly in Armadale where they had relatively few alternative activities within the town. As many as 32% of the boys of the whole sample and 19% of the girls reckoned to go to a cafe twice or more a week while 44% and 33% respectively had been at least once in the previous seven days (Table 23). In Drumchapel about one in four had been at a cafe although it had involved them in another bus journey unless they had stayed down town after work. The boys made rather more use of cafes than the girls but neither age nor educational level was relevant. The youngsters were extremely knowledgeable about the cafes near and far. Four Drumchapel girls rattled off in a matter of minutes the names of 15 cafes in Clydebank, Anniesland and the city centre. They could also pin its social character onto any one of them—'usually a lot of rough folk go there', or 'the G—, that's just for snobs.' Availability, of course, is one reason why the youngsters use cafes so extensively. Open early and late and often for seven days in the week, the cafe can be fitted into the rigid timetables of job, school and evening class. It also has important social assets. You can take your new friend to a cafe without, as with a youth group, the embarrassment of having to introduce him to some adult or expose him to the risk of being asked to *do* something. Juke box and radio make the place cheerful. The small tables or partitions suggest an intimate atmosphere while still allowing one to eye the rest of the room. The cafe is very much the youngster's own world. As a group of apprentices pointed out, you can swear at your ease in a place where there is neither a bunch of weans nor a lot of old people. A nice, cosy rounder-off of the evening's main event, the cafe also has the prime virtue that it is cheap.

The youngsters were questioned closely as to whether they thought that cafe-going, however enjoyable, was basically a waste of time. Those—the minority—who were critical argued that young people only went to cafes if they were fed up or so dim that they could not find other interests. Other critics saw 'cafe-boys' as different and inferior to 'sporty boys'. One wrote that 'Morals are easily lowered in a cafe' and another said ominously 'It's when the cafes are closed that things happen.' Though some argued against cafe-going on the ground that fights start there, it was significant that they made far less reference to Trouble in connection with cafes than with dancing. The great majority were strongly in favour and it was interesting that they made their case less on grounds of enjoyment or cheapness than because of the cafe's social assets. Cafes helped you to meet new people which they saw as an essential part of growing up. You could exchange ideas more readily there than at the street corner or when just walking around. It is perhaps worth quoting the views of one of the older boys, an apprentice shipwright. Though not much of a cafe-goer himself, being more interested in pubs, pools and snooker, he nevertheless put 'cafe' as Drumchapel's major need. The following week's diary shows the part cafe-going may play in a youngster's life.

Tuesday: Went to cafe on the way home from school. Had a look through some of the work that one of the girls from the crowd that go to the cafe had with her. . . . Persuaded dad to let me out to the cafe tonight. One of the boys brought in to the cafe the new book written by Spike Milligan. We spent half the night killing ourselves laughing at some of the catch lines in it.

Wednesday: Stayed in, did homework, and watched the T.V.

Thursday: Went into the cafe on the way home from school and discussed the happenings of the day and the teachers we had that day, and what we would do at the week-end. . . . After tea, and after a long persuasive moan at my father, I went out to another cafe since the —— shuts on a Thursday. . . . Most of the crowd from the —— stay in on a Thursday so I went to the —— and met some other school friends and we talked. . . .

Friday: Got my pocket money today but just went to the cafe where I made up with my girl friend again (we had had an argument on Monday). I was late again because I took too long in seeing L— home.

Saturday: Went along to the cafe in the afternoon and collected a few compliments about my jacket's latest mod cut. . . .

Sunday: Went to the cafe in the evening after I had finished my swotting. . . . I just sat in the cafe all night and then walked L— home.

Monday: Swotted at home.

The last four activities asked about under Leisure II were spectator sport, ten-pin bowling, ice skating and pub-going. The youngsters took much less part in any of these than they did in the cinema-dancing-cafe syndrome (Table 22). Spectator sport was practically confined to football and to the boys. Only 5% referred to it and only 24 individuals had taken part in the previous seven days. At the time the study was starting there was a lot of talk about ten-pin bowling, which was why it was asked about by name at the interview. But the numbers in the sample who did anything about it proved negligible. A visit to the Bowl at the new town of East Kilbride also showed that relatively few of the many adolescents present were actually bowling. Perhaps the cost was prohibitive or were they impatient of the long queues? Low numbers were also recorded for ice skating since only 7% referred to it and only 16 individuals had been skating in the previous seven days. The Armadale boys and girls, who had an 8-mile journey to their nearest (Falkirk) rink, had a higher proportion of skaters than had either of the other areas. Presumably the key was the special Saturday skaters' buses which collect from various parts of Midlothian.

The final activity listed in Leisure II was pub-going. Since the majority of the youngsters were under age as regards pub-going their comments were probably guarded however much the interviewer tried to equate his questions with cafe-going.

Then too, some interviews were held within parental earshot and some parents disapproved of pubs irrespective of a youngster's age. Thus the figures may be an understatement. On the other hand some reliability is suggested by the fact that the area ones relating to boys' visits to pubs during the last seven days were fairly constant—12% for Dennistoun, 13% for Drumchapel and 10% for Armadale (Table 21). Dennistoun and Drumchapel were also much alike for the girls' answers, 5% and 4% respectively. The negligible figure for Armadale, just 1%, was to be expected in a small community where pub-going for women is likely to be frowned on. Points to note are the small proportion who said they used pubs compared to the cafe-goers, and the little set, 3% of those aged 15-17½, who were prepared to admit that they went to pubs.

Formal groups (Leisure connected with membership of a formal group including those of the Youth Service)

The fourth main type of leisure necessitated membership of a formal group. The term was defined very loosely in that it included groups which catered for all ages and interests, from drama, pigeon, and sports clubs (apart from those covered by Leisure I and II) to units of such organisations as the Youth Hostels Association, the Campaign for Nuclear Disarmament or the Orange Lodge. Any group within the Youth Service was included.[13] Though expected to be numerically important they were not classed separately since a characteristic of 'formal group' as one of the provisions for young people's leisure is the fact of belonging, not the nature of the group's interests. The interviewers paid particularly careful attention to the use made of formal groups and tried to make certain that any membership they recorded was, in fact, a live one. The figures in Table 24 (which may well have included overlapping membership) show that only 21% belonged to formal groups ('Sports clubs, other formal groups and additional formal group') *other* than those of the Youth Service; and that rather less than half of the membership to non-Youth Service groups

[13] Membership of groups connected with the Church were classified as follows. If worship was the group's prime purpose it was listed as 'Church service' in Table 24. If it functioned chiefly on social grounds, it was included in formal groups in general. Thus membership of a youth fellowship was included in formal groups but not that of a Sunday school.

was to sports clubs as such. In view of the extent to which the Youth Service units dominated the figures relating to formal groups, the material in the following paragraphs deals very largely with groups associated with the Service.

The most reliable figure in Table 24, since it avoids the risk of overlapping membership, is that of the 61% who did not belong.[14] No marked association with sex, age or area was apparent. Current educational situation was, however, very relevant: those still in full-time education (and it will be remembered that all had stayed on voluntarily) were much more likely to belong to a formal group than those at work. Of the boys in full-time education 41% were non-members; of the boys at work 68%. The discrepancy was still more marked in the case of the girls. Of those in full-time education 31% were non-members, of those at work 66%. Area differences were less than might have been expected. Dennistoun, despite a higher proportion than the other areas of youngsters still in full-time education, still had 57% of non-members, Drumchapel 61% and Armadale 67%. For the Armadale girls the figure reached 72%. It was impossible for the sample as a whole to relate level of education to membership because no detailed information was available about the standard of those who had attended comprehensive schools. But as hardly any of the non-joiners in Armadale and Dennistoun had been at this type of school, a limited analysis was possible. Non-joiners comprised 67% of the Armadale, and 57% of the Dennistoun sample. Fifty per cent of the Armadale and 35% of the Dennistoun non-joiners had a junior secondary education, 15% and 19% respectively a senior secondary one. As regards the type of group joined, and referring only to the first four in Table 24, youth clubs headed the list. The 11% of boys in uniformed organisations should be noted.

The actual attendance at formal groups is shown in Table 25.

[14] Though comparisons of membership figures are dangerous the following may be of interest.

(*a*) (1942) 'Not shown in full-time Education for Approved Activity at time of Registration—58·9%.' *Youth Registration in Scotland* 1942 (relates to age 16 only).

(*b*) (1950) 'Membership of an organised social group—41·3%' ∴ non-membership = 58·7%. *op. cit.* Ferguson and Cunnison. (Relates to Glasgow boys who left school at 14 and were 17 at the date to which membership refers.)

In the last seven days the 232 joiners had made 201 attendances which is a high figure since there was no certainty that all the groups of which they were members had, in fact, held a meeting during the previous seven days. Another indication of good use was shown in the answers to a question on how often they reckoned to go. Only 9% went irregularly which, incidentally, confirmed that any membership they had referred to was probably an active one. As many as 14% went twice or more times per week, the boys being more intensive users than the girls.

No attempt was made to assess statistically what advantages accrued to the youngster through belonging to a formal group. But one of the 18-year-old boys probably put his finger on the heart of the matter in the final words of something he wrote in another connection.

If I would have had better education and Money I would have liked to have gone to Canada or some place Abord but fears I got my Brother to send for Imagration papers once but I was afrad to fill them In because I got in trouble with the ploice. And I was afrad if I fill them in I get a big let down and ever since then I came tow the youth Club and nearly forget about my fears because there all very friendly.

Why did nearly two in three make no use of the opportunities for leisure provided through formal groups and in particular through those of the Youth Service? They gave a gamut of reasons for not joining and when asked to describe any non-joiner (aged 15-19) they knew personally it was noticed that they described individuals of very different types. A boy of 17 drew the following pen-picture of one real life non-joiner.

He is very fashion conscious. He likes to dress in the present craze for 'gear'. There is a close relationship between us as he is my brother. His family, and mine ... well they don't exist outside myself and two younger brothers: my mother and father died 6 yrs. ago and we have since lived in about 6 children's homes.

J.M. likes to brag about his girl-friends and companions. I studied his friends and they are all shallow, insecure and over indulgent in frivolous pastime—I know because I often joined in when we went out with the 'birds'. Why did I go out with these people? Well like J.M. (my brother) I was impressed by the bragging they did and thought I would see how much of it was truth. All of it was. They have no time for youth organisations, they look down on them as kid's stuff. J.M. does not go around picking fights but his general behaviour suggests part-hooliganism. He detests school pupils of any age and thinks they are all 'weirdos'. This causes arguments between us and he sticks to his guns vehemently, believing himself to be a mature man. We are both living digs at the moment but J.M. joins the army on Sunday. He hates dirty Jokes, I love them provided they are genuinely funny. I can not claim to be all saint.

Another boy (16) describing an ex-friend who was a non-joiner observed that

He comes from a very well off family. His father is a lawyer. He has no lack of money ... he is a nervous, unsure person, afraid of any type of physical risk.

And a girl (16) drew this little sketch of an individual she knew who had no use for youth organisations. The girl, she said, had

no family background. She is an orphan trying to make a decent living, although most of the time she gives up when everything gets on top of her. She has practically no money to spend on herself, as what she earns is put towards her lodgings and her keep. This kind of girl has very few friends as she cannot afford what they can afford, she cannot buy what they can buy and as a result her night's entertainment would be to sit cuddled by the fire reading a book of some sort. Her clothes are limited to the bare necessities, one dress, one skirt and one blouse. She enjoys one thing and that is her work, which consists of type-writing and shorthand, gained by endless weeks at night classes. Due to her poverty, she had to leave school at fifteen without any training for a job, but with her determination to go on, eventually gained a worth while job. She detests having to live alone, and is very much afraid of the future. Will it always be like this she wonders, what is the point of living when life is hard and lonely and comes to a point when its unbearable.

The youngsters' reasons for not joining formal groups, however nebulous and interlocking, were on the whole associated with the group's structure rather than its activities. Whatever its type—uniformed, church-linked, Local Authority-run—the group tended to have an over-authoritarian flavour. Typical comment was that 'You are too much bossed around', 'that youth leaders like ... all the things their own way'; that 'all major decisions are taken by ministers and elders'; and that 'if I put any suggestions forward I am told "just belt up" '. Another writer wanted 'a place which makes young people feel they are needed and not there to obey an older person's orders'. In some cases what sounded like a leaden ring about the words 'youth organisation' was possibly related to the fact that the speaker was being over-controlled at school or in his job. This continual reference to the dislike of being bossed around seemed to be associated with their experience of large communities and the almost inevitable rigidity associated with over-sized classes at school and big impersonal groups at work.

It was the less bright and the less articulate who could not get *their* ideas and *their* wants across except in quite small and face-to-face situations. Is it also just possible that today's adolescent inherits more than the normal reluctance to being regimented from a generation of fathers who had a surfeit of external control in the Forces? The youngsters' argument that in your free time nothing ought to be compulsory was accompanied by the charge that so often in a youth organisation you *had* to take part in activities. Quite apart from the question of imposed authority, their comment suggested that they wanted a group which, first and foremost, would give them the opportunity to be with other youngsters, only secondly to do things. Some of the youth groups saw this as indolence and certain units laid down that when present one must be obviously occupied. The more socially able youngster, who was likely to be the better educated one, took this in his stride and probably enjoyed the challenge; the less competent or less self-assured would not risk the chance of failure.

Many of the boys and girls were convinced that any organisation which was even loosely linked with education would inevitably be run on authoritarian lines. 'School', with its discipline and emphasis on work, did not suggest much likelihood of the enjoyment to which they felt entitled in their free time. His job and the extra money in his pocket gives the ex-school child a status that he is not going to jeopardise by going back to anything associated with school. Other relevant comment was that 'You are given the impression that you are not wanted in school'; that 'Teachers get a feeling of grandeur because they can order us about'; and that 'Teachers are machines... who never really understood (us)'. In view of all this criticism of school why, as was shown earlier, did those still in full-time education join groups more than did those who had left school? Presumably the answer is connected with the fact that in the sample on which this study was based all who were still at school had stayed on voluntarily. This probably means that even if they had not done particularly well there they were not actively hostile to it. Moreover, as youngsters still at school, they were being daily conditioned by this world that offered them things which they were expected to accept as a matter of routine. Teachers also point out that the senior secondary school child is more prone than the one at a junior school to develop a passion for some particular activity. All told, therefore, the youngsters still in full-time education are that much more likely than those at work not only to accept, but deliberately to go after the facilities offered by the formal group.

Another set of the reasons which the boys and girls gave for not joining youth organisations was the groups' association with the Church. This was rather unexpected in view of the fairly high proportion of the sample who had an active link with the Church. Examples of comment were as follows. A 17-year-old boy, writing of what he thought would be useful for leisure wanted

> A large youth centre open on a Sunday with the same activities as during the week and on Saturdays including dancing, table tennis and snooker but without religion as at all the youth clubs you get lectures on it there is a time and a place for everything and when teenagers enjoy themselves it is not the time for religion.

The Church was dull and ministers 'elderly men talking of things that happened thousands of years ago'. Or again, 'Ministers say prayers and speeches and half the time you fall asleep they talk that slow and dreary way. I would like my time spent going to dancing, clubs, cafes, pictures.' The considered comments of one of the older girls, a 19-year-old manual worker, were worth noting. She said that deep down she and her circle of friends were interested in religion and felt a bit guilty about not going to a church. But the set-up was so formal that it demanded different clothes from the ones you went out in at night. Secondly, the same things happened over and over again at church. It was dreary. Thirdly, the adults always overcontrolled the church youth groups. Also you got kidded by your contemporaries if you went to church. A stereotype about church and social class which was frequently encountered was that church-goers considered themselves above the ordinary run of people. This alleged link between church and social class, if length of education may still be regarded as one aspect of class, was examined for membership of youth fellowships as recorded in the sample. Of those who belonged to a fellowship 41% were in full-time education compared with the 18% in the sample as a whole. Quite another type of reason for not joining any church-linked group was when the youngster's family had no connection with a church. If his parents had given up church-going they probably did not encourage and support him in his membership as was often seen to be the case with the youngster in the church-linked family.

The formal groups of the Youth Service were also dismissed as being over-juvenile. Few of those visited in the course of this study gave the impression of being adult enough for the boy who, by 17 or so, already had a couple of years' experience of working alongside men in a rough unskilled job. A boy of 17 summed up the widespread belief about the juvenile character of most youth organisations when he criticised them as 'removed from life in their views on public morality, alcoholism and other major talking points of this day and age.' Certain of the older girls had no use at all for youth groups because they would only find in them boys of their own age or under it, not the fellows in their early twenties whom they wanted to meet. Criticism from the younger adolescents, those of 15 and 16, was mostly linked with the point referred to earlier, viz. that they associated youth groups with school which was a

FIG. 9. Club art class, Drumchapel

world they had grown beyond. Many of the adults also regarded youth organisations as basically a provision for children which is, of course, the case when their *total* membership is taken into account. For instance, the 1965-6 returns from the Scottish Education Department for the 31 major youth organisations show that nearly as many of the members were under 12 as between 12 and 21. Examination of the teenage membership of the Girl Guides Association (chosen because of the admirably detailed figures it always provides) showed that in 1964 there was a recession in membership for each age year between 13 and 19 with a very considerable decline between 14 and 15. By 15 the largest number had left.[15] Though the situation differs considerably in areas and individual companies this is the national picture which determines the popular image. Another attempt to see why so many adults associated youth groups with children rather than adolescents was by noting the age structure of those attending the Youth Service clubs and centres of the Education Authority in the two Glasgow study areas. The age of those actually present during the few weeks examined showed that in 5 of the 8 sets of figures available, more than half of the youngsters were aged 14 and under; in the other 3 sets a third or more were under 14[16]

Another of the reasons why the adolescents did not make more

[15] *Girl Guides Association (Scotland)*. Census. 1966.

Age	Numbers in this age group as % of total aged 13-19
13	39
14	27
15	14
16	6
17	5
18	5
19	4

[16] *Glasgow Corporation Further Education Evening Centres and Clubs*. One week's attendance in relation to age (March and April 1965).

Centre or club	Percentage of attenders aged 14 and under	
	Boys	Girls
(a) Further Education centre	60	57
(b) Further Education centre	47	77
(c) Further Education centre	32	71
(d) Youth club	45	72

Note: The weeks concerned were towards the end of the spring session when attendance was below average. But this would be unlikely to affect the age structure.

use of the youth groups was that they were less available than many other types of leisure. The majority of the voluntary organisation groups only reckoned to function once a week and there were often lengthy gaps even in this. Any group linked with school or which used school premises did not normally meet when the school was on holiday. Taking week-ends into account the schools are shut for the equivalent of 17-18 weeks, or about a third of the year. The youth groups also made many complaints about having to be out of school premises by 10 p.m., a very early hour for adolescents if understandable from the point of view of the janitor's hours of duty. Few groups except those definitely associated with a church provided any leisure facilities for Sunday, a day on which homes are full, cash is short and many types of recreation not available. Sunday morning's long lie in bed was perhaps no more due to late nights on Friday and Saturday than a way of shortening a day that would be dull anyhow. And practically no groups catered for the youngster with unusual hours such as the bakery machine boy who worked an 11 p.m.-6.30 a.m. shift one week, a 9.10 a.m.-9.30 p.m. the next.

Availability was also lessened by the long break in the summer which was a feature of most of the organisations. As said before, the 17 or 18 weeks of the school holidays were dead as far as voluntary organisations using indoor school premises were concerned. Local Authority youth groups stopped their indoor and main programmes from mid-April to mid-September and many closed entirely from mid-June onwards. Except for outdoor activities, no Authority-provided staff were available in the summer. Even a very active organisation like the Boys' Brigade had this long gap, an example being the five companies working in Dennistoun. Apart from three which ran a one-week camp, all five were shut from, at latest, mid-May to the first week in September (1965). A long period without any meetings had two added disadvantages. If the group functioned for only a few weeks after Easter it probably did not bother to get a summer programme going, and when it did re-open in September it might have to rebuild more or less from scratch. In the case of youngsters who are still at school a relevant point is that homework tends to ease off after the Easter exams so that this is a time when they have that much more need of leisure facilities. While this long summer closure is a welcome break to the adults in charge of groups it is worth remembering that adolescents live on a shorter time-scale than adults. Also many do not go away for an annual holiday (not much more than half of the sample did so). Lastly there is the point that the holiday months get a lot of rain: in 1962, 1963 and 1964 the second wettest month of the year for Scotland was August.

There was some demand, especially from those who had left school, for more groups devoted to a single interest. The boys and girls in question were definitely bright individuals, moving up socially through their jobs and perhaps more able to concentrate than the 'average' youngster. They had scant use for anything as juvenile or dull-sounding as a recreational evening class and they sheered off any group likely to be dominated by adults. Something akin to the societies which a student population produces would probably have suited them.

To sum up. The broad picture derived from the interviews was that the boys and girls spent a very considerable proportion of their leisure doing nothing in particular. This was especially true of the many hours which they spent in their own homes. Three main types of commercial provision for leisure—cinema, dancing and cafe—had high priority in the youngsters' eyes and in the amount of time they devoted to them. Sport, a common interest among the boys, attracted little attention from the girls. The range of activities on which leisure was spent was limited. No very considerable use was made of formal groups of any type. Of those provided by the Youth Service, the reluctance to join appeared to be more associated with the group's structure than with the nature of its activities. The above negative picture was offset by a strong impression that a very considerable proportion of the adolescents were on the brink of using their time in more diverse and lively ways though they themselves had few clear-cut ideas as to what precisely they wanted. Given more generous and imaginative facilities (which were urgently needed) just a little push might have done the trick provided it was on a personal basis and sustained for a time. This push was particularly necessary in the case of those who had no more than a junior secondary education. By and large these were the adolescents who did not go after things for themselves.

Chapter VI

SOME OF THE VIEWS EXPRESSED BY THE
BOYS AND GIRLS

Most of the 3,000 or so youngsters who were consulted about their spare time in the various ways described in Chapter IV had views to air. Some of this comment was used in the preceding chapter to elaborate the plain facts provided by the 600 who were actually interviewd. A more detailed account of their views, especially as these emerged in discussion groups, written material and drawings, is given in this chapter. These views prove nothing in a quantitative way. All they do is illustrate what *some* boys and girls in this 15-19 age group thought about *some* of the subjects which bore on how they chose to spend their free time.

Personal relationships, 'my friend', played an important role in leisure, particularly in the case of the girls. This special friend was rather more likely to be of the same than of the opposite sex. At least half of the girls referred to their girl friend, a third of the boys to their mate. There was some indication that a friend of one's own sex provided an easier relationship for the less mature youngster to handle than did the 'my boy' or 'my girl' whom commercial pressures suggest every self-respecting adolescent ought to acquire. Certain of the girls had a lot to put up with from a bosom friend who, less mature than themselves, anchored over-closely. As regards a friend of the opposite sex this probably mattered more to the girls than it did to their brothers. 'My boy' was a status symbol and possibly gave the security that the girls from junior secondary schools often lacked. In addition to the special friend their group of friends was, of course, a vital factor in the leisure of most of the youngsters. They disparaged anyone who constantly changed his friend(s) and strongly approved of loyalty to the group.

Where to look for nice boys was a problem for many of the girls. The older Drumchapel girls complained that one had to go outside the estate to meet young men in their 20's, yet another reflection of Drumchapel's abnormal population structure. One of the snags of youth groups as a hunting ground for a boy or girl friend was that so often the group required one to take part in various activities before, or as well as, using it to meet personal needs. Part of the trouble with commercial provision in relation to courting was the expense. Plenty of promising romances were nipped in the bud because the boy could not afford to keep up a favourable start made at the week-end until his next pay-day. The popularity of parties as a place to meet potential new friends seemed to be associated partly with courting needs. They afforded a recognised setting for petting. But not all spirits soared at the mention of a party and in any case the number of parties was limited. Courting had a marked influence on leisure in that those who were going steady reckoned to spend a large amount of their time in each other's company. One typical example was a 17-year-old clerkess who tried to meet her boy five nights a week and was with him and his family, perhaps at the pictures or out in the car, on Saturdays. A small Edinburgh study made by a group of the Young Christian Workers and relating to 71 people in the 15-25 age group showed that over half of those who were engaged or had a steady friend spent four or more nights in the week together.

It may be worth noting a few of the points which came out in the study on the needs of girls. They seemed much less reluctant than the boys to follow a lead as regards their leisure or, indeed, their life in general. Many of them really preferred to have someone take them by hand. They followed other girls, longed to be like everyone else, and had little confidence in themselves. They enjoyed talking to other girls and needed opportunities for this. Though they wanted to meet boys—'a girl is always happier when she is going with a boy, that is when she's at her best'—they were not at ease with groups of relatively strange boys and often preferred to be with just one. On occasion they wanted to do something mad, like driving a fast car or swimming in Loch Lomond. They often felt they should *do* more but somehow the mere presence of adults held them back.

'Relationships between the sexes' was a matter which the boys and girls were always ready to discuss. The phrase tended to be interpreted as the sex relationship only and this had to be thrashed out at length before they could discuss anything wider. The Drumchapel group would have talked about sex in all its ramifications week after week to the exclusion of almost anything else. They valued the opportunity which this discussion afforded to learn from each other about the opposite sex. Some of the boys felt that this talk uncovered certain of the secrets about women and that this would be handy in their competition for girls. That boys too could be shy, or could admire girls for things other than their looks, was news to a good many of the girls. In other words this group talk helped to dispel stereotypes and startled the youngsters into seeing each other less as talent to be chased or as boys to be lured than as persons in their own right. Practical matters—the best age at which to marry or the financial side of marriage—occupied their minds as well as romance and love. Another subject they wanted to discuss, partly through curiosity, partly because it constituted a real threat, was homosexuality. They knew the words but were often vague as to their precise meaning.

Examples of the above views, taken from notes made by the adult recorders at two of the discussion groups, read as follows. The first notes, from a group of 5 boys aged about $17\frac{1}{2}$, read:

Many boys go round saying that they have stuffed this one and that one but wouldn't stuff their own girl. 'Boys only want one thing' the girls say. The boys say that the girls expect you to try something. If you don't they are surprised. 'Girls need us as much as we do them.' Girls don't talk so much of sex—they have to wait till the boy comes. Boys like someone who has a bit of fight in her: they don't want it too easy. 'A nice girl is one who doesn't go easily'. (Talk on girls who work in hospitals and seem to have a lot of sex.) You mustn't go at them too quick. Don't like you going for it first time. Got to play your cards nonchalantly. Girls need sex—their needs are greater. Once a boy is satisfied, that's that, but girls take longer to work up and finish later. Girls want the romantic aspect of it. One boy tried 'Spanish Fly' (as an aphrodisiac) in a girl's drink but didn't work: reckons it was sand. Girls need something to occupy their minds—domestic things. Girls tend to follow whatever you are talking about.

Another example of typical discussion, from a group of 7 boys aged about 17, read:

The boys suggested (as an excuse perhaps for promiscuous habits) that a girl wanted a man with experience. Further comment about girls was that if you get a lassie of 16 who's a virgin, it's the exception. One boy started at the age of 11 with his younger brother and 'jumped about' with wee lassies. Another told of how at the age of 9 he had been initiated by a girl of 16 who had taken him and a number of other wee boys into a close. 'After that', says he, 'I never looked back'. When I asked if they ever thought of a girls' feelings at such a time they said that they mostly went out to satisfy themselves but occasionally to try and satisfy the girl. One said that one night he'd been with a virgin and that while he was satisfying himself she was screaming away—he added that he felt sorry for that one. On occasions they had been out with girls who didn't want to do it. However, if a lassie gave in to their advances, they didn't hold back.

The youngsters were very open in their talk on pre-marital intercourse. There was not much evidence that they regarded this as a thing to worry about. Indeed they thought adults more bothered on their behalf than they were themselves. But they gave the impression that they certainly did not think pre-marital intercourse should be encouraged. They seemed to be arguing not on moral grounds but because they saw risks to the child who is illegitimate and, to a lesser degree, to the unmarried mother. As to what proportion thought pre-marital intercourse 'all right', it is unlikely that the code to which these Scottish adolescents subscribed would vary much from that followed by their contemporaries in other parts of Britain. Mr Schofield's detailed study, based on samples of 15-19 age populations in England, shows that it would be a mistake to assume that most youngsters of this age are sexually experienced.[1] One small Scottish study, undertaken in 1965 by the Social Psychology Department of the University of Glasgow and based on a 5% quota sample of students, showed that about half (44% men, 59% women) of this more mature and more sophisticated age group considered pre-marital intercourse to be socially undesirable.[2]

The boys and girls gave a strong impression of being serious about their relationships with the opposite sex. They were not just a bunch of youngsters who were out for a good time. They quite obviously valued the opportunity to talk among themselves but with someone at hand who had rather more experience of life. They were also ready to think about the wider issues once these were brought to their attention, e.g. that the relationship between the sexes is a more fundamental and exciting matter than the sex relationship as such. Some of them, disheartened about not doing too well in the courting stakes, badly needed the reassurance which comes from the

[1] *The Sexual Behaviour of Young People.* Schofield. Longmans, 1965.
[2] *Glasgow University Undergraduates' Attitudes to Marriage,* 1965 (unpublished study).

knowledge that individuals mature at different rates. The girls might have been saved many heartbreaks and the impulsive actions that spring from them if they had been helped to come to terms with the hard fact that, by and large, boys 'are for any, not one but the many'. With marriage more imminent now than in the past, they plainly should be given more information about the social risks involved in very early marriage (p. 137).

The way in which the youngsters used their leisure was, of course, coloured by their views on adult society. As regards parents, their closest relationship with the adult world, they gave the impression that they wanted to be on good terms with older people despite mutual moanings. Their writings and what was seen of the Leavers in their own homes confirmed this. Typical attitudes were the following:

Older people do not understand the easy-going attitude of teenagers. When something goes wrong, older people get all ruffled, and expect teenagers to do the same. I see no reason why teenagers should fret and worry when things go wrong. Also older people do not realise that when young people reach the age of 16-18 they begin to want a little independence, but find this difficult sometimes, due to possessive parents, to very strict rules at school or work. As a result they become restless and irritable.

The next comment is from a discussion group where the participants were aged 17 and 18.

Parents lose a lot of imagination as they grow older because more materialistic. Teenagers have more ideas. Parents hide ideas of sex—deny it. . . . Parents disapprove of drink as they know the ill-effects. They want to protect you from making the same mistakes. Parents should be stricter on many things. Young folk should be careful if not good. It's more important not to get caught. (But not all agreed with this.) Parents often try to make you come home early—just something to moan about. Most people suit themselves. Don't listen to parents any longer. They always want gratitude for all they have done for you. But parents have great things to offer. Even their views rub off on you through time. Usually you realise too late that they were right. (*How would you advise parents?*) Would advise them on clothes, style. Could help them smarten up a bit. Don't want them bang up to date but they should have nice, well-cut suits. Shouldn't wear suits for ten years. Got to help them out of conservative thinking—show them the short-cuts to doing things. They're still obsessed with the war—it was their only glory. Parents could ask their kids for advice now and again. Can't advise them on sex and love. Would take parents out for a drink etc. but they wouldn't come. When they get a couple of drinks they sing *Nellie Dean* etc.—their songs are far behind us. Still we can't keep moving with the times—got to stop sometime. Old people have had their fun—they're quite happy with the way things are—like to have their wee routines.

The above group also quoted examples of parental bad behaviour which had disgusted them, such as the mother who was too drunk to watch her children. Though strongly opposed to what they considered were over-authoritarian attitudes, they sometimes criticised their parents for not holding them on a tighter rein. A case in point was the girl who said that she wished her mother bothered enough about her to see that she did come home at night after a party. They also pointed out that if parents did not happen to enjoy the same kind of leisure as their children did, they condemned it wholesale. A parent could be a real embarrassment to an adolescent—'My mum's that *fat*.' It was plain, too, that some parents did not trouble to find out what fantasy image of a father or mother their older children had in mind. The youngsters criticised adults as being over-ready to equate harmless matters but ones terribly important to themselves, e.g. mod gear, with anti-social behaviour. A point which came out repeatedly was their criticism of the thoughtless way in which the adult world linked anyone who happened to be an adolescent with Trouble. The youngsters were quite prepared to admit that they themselves were far from perfect. 'I don't blame older people', wrote one boy, 'I don't know how they stand all the cheek they get.' This was typical of their willingness to be honest about themselves.

On the whole they gave the impression of being slightly sorry for, rather than hostile to the adult world. They found grown ups a dull lot, bogged down in the 'dreary desert sand of dead habit'. It also looked as if many of these adolescents had few friendly contacts with adults apart from those of their family circle. Most of those they met regularly tended to be in authority—the foreman, the teacher, the minister. The discussion group youngsters were surprised to find the adults whom they encountered there so human. Since a breakdown in relationships between the adolescent and older people is one of the features of 'unattached' youngsters,[3] there is a strong case for increasing the opportunities for contact. Part of the problem is lack of informal meeting places which the generations can use on equal terms. The pub is not available for those under 18 and in any case one does not want to encourage youngsters to use a meeting place which is centred on drinking.

[3] *The Unattached*. Morse. Pelican, 1965.

Teachers, of course, were among the adults with whom the boys and girls had had first hand and continuous contact. Though summed up as 'not all that bad', there was little evidence that teachers were the kind of adults they admired. They had no strong feelings against them for using the belt but they plainly despised the belt-happy teacher—it was an admission of defeat. But many were discontented about their past schooling and in particular with the competitive element—grading, marks, and so on. Girls who had been put into classes which they felt their teachers had regarded as 'no good' had not bothered to work any more. Dislike of school seemed to be strongly associated with having been allowed to believe that their teachers thought poorly of them. Another set, those not actively anti-school, had obviously not found anything there which had really excited their interest. Both these reactions came up time and again and were relevant to this study since they hindered the youngster from attempting to use his leisure in unfamiliar ways or under conditions that he remotely associated with school.

Their comments on another aspect of adult society, the Church, related more often to its function as a social institution than to religion as concerned with worship. The adults of this study did not know any of the youngsters well enough to talk freely about the deeper issues. Forty-three per cent of the sample had regular association with a church[4] (Table 24); as many as 1 in 3 had taken part in some kind of religious activity in the previous seven days. In this connection it should be recalled that, judging from their former or current school, 1 in 5 of the youngsters came from a Roman Catholic home. They said that they talked about religion quite a lot at work, and the discussion groups certainly suggested that religion was one of the matters in which they were interested. Positive views (that of a girl who said she had 'found God a great comfort') were less often mentioned than negative ones (that of the 15-year old who wrote off religion as 'a lot of rubbish', or of a boy who was said to have 'no faith in anything except money'). Many found the Church old-fashioned and out of touch. It was also no place for anyone of their age—*kids* went to Sunday School, *old* people to church. It was probably on some such grounds rather than antagonism to religion that

[4] See reference 13 to chapter V.

certain youngsters and their parents advised the team not to use church premises when starting a new discussion group. The youngsters also associated the Church with social class distinctions though the ones who actually belonged to a church organisation disputed this. Sectarianism, the Protestant/Catholic line-up, was still a live issue. They were, of course, at an age when it was beginning to involve them in serious problems connected with their personal relationships. Despite the considerable proportion who had a definite link with the Church, they mostly left its own teaching out of the picture when discussing what they felt were real problems like sex relationships or stealing. Queer distorted notions about religion and the Church were fairly common. 'Riddled with daft ideas' was a comment from one of the discussion group recorders. They urgently needed to talk with people who would help them sort things out while they were young enough to be receptive to new ideas.

How far did these boys and girls take an interest in public affairs? Most had neither the experience of life nor the education to think in terms other than the personal and the issues they saw as important were concrete matters which bore directly on their own life. On the other hand, the T.V., and to a lesser extent the daily press, now bring news of public affairs into every type of home and they attracted some attention from the most illiterate of the boys and girls. But on the whole these youngsters did not feel themselves involved. A couple of lively groups in which a dozen youngsters of 16-18 took part did not care if they got the vote at 18 or not. They thought vaguely that the bomb should be banned. Coloured people were all right though personally they would not go out with a coloured person. As regards their own future, they did not envisage this as differing much from that of their parents. They spoke in terms of marriage, a set number of children, a nice home and a secure job. There was some talk of emigrating, chiefly to Australia, and a marked interest in travel, particularly among the girls of 17 or so. On the other hand if it was a question of spending £35 for a couple of weeks on the Continent as opposed to buying a stylish summer coat, the latter won (as far as one 17-year-old boy was concerned). In view of their rather stereotyped aspirations about their own future, one would expect them to develop the same fairly traditional outlook on politics which was noted in a recent study on young voters.[5]

The youngsters' views on another aspect of adult society came out in their attitude to their jobs, their earnings, and how they spent their money. Before commenting it may be of interest to quote what three individuals wrote in answer to the question 'Money can get you anything. What do you think?'

It is my belief that money with the exception of health can obtain for you anything. Without money one in this modern age is lost. The pastimes of our parents like walks and picnics have died out because of the money we have and places we can go. Even love, not just sex, can be bought at a price and money today is a tyrant for example a man with plenty of money can hire others to do anything he wishes even going to the extreme of murder. Therefore I believe that, as I have said before, with the exception of incurable diseases money can procure any desire of man whatsoever.

Money can buy most things necessary for happiness—Money buys freedom from care, even friends, maybe not true friends but companions in leisure activities. If asked to choose between two attractive men, I would choose the one with most money. Life is too short to spend any moment worrying about financial circumstances.

Money can get you plenty of things but look at it this way money can't get you to heaven, it doesn't always give you happiness, your mother could be dying but you just couldn't say to the doctor 'here's £100 I want my mother out of bed by next week'.

Though very conscious of the costs of leisure, the boys and girls gave the impression that money was not all that important to them. There was little indication that they tried to change jobs for financial reasons and even the apprentices did not make many complaints about their very low earnings. Parents were more inclined to be critical than the boys themselves. Clothes and personal appearance was extremely important and formed one of the leisure-time fillers which they pursued consistently and skilfully without any adult prodding, apart from the impersonal pressures of the commercial world. Some boys even listed 'clothes' as their chief hobby. A lot of steady thought, discussion and money went on mod gear, shoes, cosmetics—mascara, eye liner, eye shadow, pan stick. Another regular field of spending was connected with pop and canned music. Cafe life was another thing on which they reckoned to spend regularly. So were the pleasures of the week-end. A couple of

[5] 'The Young Voter in British Politics'. Abrams and Little. *The British Journal of Sociology*. Vol. XVI No. 2, June 1965.

16-year-old Drumchapel girls costed their Friday night routine at Dennistoun Palais as tickets 5/-, cloakroom 3d, cokes 1/3, cigarettes 2/2, fares 2/- 'and still Saturday to pay for'. Fares might add as much as one-third to the cost of many of the accepted types of leisure. This was resented as utterly unproductive. In general, however, their outlook on money was refreshingly unmercenary. Many of the younger ones seemed content with 'enough cash for the weekend and enough left over to last through next week'. As one put it 'When we have no money we just carry on to pass the time.' It was mostly the older ones, especially those contemplating marriage, who were seriously concerned with making money and keeping down the costs of their leisure. If all this seems to run counter to the amount of overtime and Saturday work taken on, it must be remembered that though overtime is nominally voluntary the junior may not like to refuse it. Perhaps, too, their programme for the Monday to Thursday evenings was not sufficiently attractive to offer any strong alternative to work. A final comment is that these youngsters at the initial stages of their career made little spontaneous reference to their jobs or to the adults they worked with. It looked as if these older people were not taking much interest in them.

Another aspect of the boys' and girls' relations with adult society came under the generic word 'Trouble'. This included vandalism, fighting, theft, housebreaking, drunkenness and a hotch-potch of offences against the officially approved codes of society. Drug-taking did not appear to be a feature of their lives. Before giving their own views on Trouble it may be useful to refer to their attitudes to drinking since they associated drink, though not necessarily drunkenness, with pleasurable leisure. They also very definitely linked it with Trouble. These youngsters, 2 in 3 of whom were aged 15-17$\frac{1}{2}$, were extremely knowledgeable about drink. Just occasionally one came across the boy who was anti-drinking and grateful for a firm parental hand—'I was really drunk and got all sorts of lectures from my mum and dad.' But most accepted drinking as an almost inevitable accompaniment of their social life. 'I drink', said a 15-year-old boy, 'Friday and Saturday so the smell goes from me before I return home. You drink twice as much Saturday because there's no work to do Sunday.' Comment from a group aged just 18 at a further education college read 'You don't feel guilt about not being 18 in a pub—how can they prove it? Some pubs serve anyone . . . if we are refused we go somewhere else.' A couple of 17-year-old boys said they had been going (to pubs) for two years just for something to do. They reckoned to drink all night. Discussion groups notes, from apprentices aged about 17, read, 'Five out of eleven do not drink, the others do so with the crowd . . . pre-dance drink is taken in moderation . . . enough to raise their courage to "get a woman" '. It was generally held that to go to a pub rather than to sit about in a cafe showed you were no longer just a wean. You were

Fig. 10. 'Trouble'

tough if you could drink, and you felt a big man if seen to be drinking. Youngsters who had been out at work long enough to be nearly accepted by adult society used drinking as an obvious way in. The girls certainly went to pubs partly as a method of moving out of the company of boys and into that of men. A surprising number of adolescents were shy and tongue-tied particularly in the presence of the opposite sex. The boys made much of the point that drink gave one self-confidence. Girls could natter away whatever company they were in, boys could not. They constantly spoke of the need to drink before going into a dance or at the early stages of a party. One 16-year-old, a poor mixer, was steeled into disastrous sociability via a half bottle of vodka brought in and tossed off in a bedroom. In general they seemed to place more importance on drink as a way of combatting feelings of inadequacy and social ill ease than on drinking as a pleasure in itself.

They could and did flout the law with little difficulty, particularly in getting drink from off-licence premises. A good deal of it came from such sources and was drunk in the street. The Drumchapel boys made much of the point that, as they had to travel out of their 'dry' housing estate to get to a pub, they drank hard in a short time. Similarly they stoked up well before a dance because they would get no more at the dance itself. They argued for a bar at dances on the ground that this meant the boys had to treat their partners, and that the additional cost, together with the presence of girls, acted as some brake on their own drinking. Naturally they drank as inexpensively as possible and they had the cheapest (and probably most potent) forms of wine. Quite young girls knew all the names—Vordo, Lanliq, etc.—and the exact price per glass and bottle.

In considering what these adolescents had to say about drinking, the following points are perhaps relevant. Such matters as affluence, the increase of leisure, alterations in the pattern of women's lives and changed relationships between the sexes have reflected themselves in drinking habits. It is socially accepted at an earlier age than formerly and there is more drinking at home. Drunkenness, too, has risen during the last ten years. One report, giving the figures for England and Wales for 1954-63, refers to a '50% increase in drunkenness ... even without any extension in the opportunities for the purchase and consumption of alcohol'.[6] The Glasgow figures for the same period also show a marked change. Individuals proceeded against for being drunk rose from 2·95 per thousand of the population (1954) to 4·42 (1963).[7] As regards juveniles, the number apprehended for being drunk and incapable were too small (itself a satisfactory sign) to show up reliable trends but the 1964 figure was markedly in excess of that for 1955. That Glasgow now has an estimated population of about 40,000 alcoholics, and that it has recently set up an information centre on alcoholism, suggests the scale of the long distance problems associated with drunkenness. The youngsters' attitudes were plainly influenced by local traditions of hard drinking and by the adult world's tacit acceptance of the fact that much of the Trouble among young people is associated with it.[8]

When this study was planned it was not envisaged that it would need to concern itself with the highly specialised subject of juvenile delinquency. But the daily comment in the press on young people and lawlessness, and the fact that some aspect or other of Trouble played so large a part in the leisure of the youngsters met with, forced attention to the subject. Time and again in the interviews the youngsters referred to Trouble. So they did in their discussion groups and, more interesting, in their written answers to questions which had no obvious bearing on the matter. In general they spoke of Trouble which had taken place in their own locality which they had either seen or heard of from friends. Relatively few were prepared to admit that they had been involved themselves. Any talk with parents who had an adolescent child also tended to veer round to Trouble. However carefully guarded against, disliked, or feared, Trouble constituted an ever present threat to the family. An example of the scale of Trouble in one of the study areas included a policeman's reference to '40 cases of housebreaking a week in this district mostly by juveniles'. Instances which the team themselves came across included a charge of attempted murder (resulting in a 5-year sentence to a Young

[6] *Decade of Drunkenness.* Prys Williams. Christian Economic and Social Research Foundation, 1965.

[7] *Report of the Chief Constable of the City of Glasgow. 1964.*

[8] 'Other ... authors believed that in the majority of cases youngsters breaking the Law under the influence of alcohol would not have done so but for the effect of alcohol in releasing aggression.' 'Crime, Alcohol and Alcoholism'. Glatt. *The Howard Journal of Penology.* Vol. XI No. 4, 1965.

Offender's Institution) by one of the 17-year-old boys who had been connected with a discussion group. One of the girl Leavers had her face slashed at a dance and an interviewer who, later on, was engaged locally on work which had no connection with the study, was threatened with a knife by 16-year-old boys on two occasions within a fortnight.

The growth of official delinquency among young people appears to be a well-documented feature of the last decade in most industrial societies. The Glasgow figures for 1964 showed that the total number of those aged 8-16 involved was nearly 13,000 (3,400 proceeded against for crimes; 5,600 proceeded against for 'all offences'; and another 3,800 brought before a Chief Superintendent for warning).[9] In the Lothians and Peebles Constabulary, which covers Armadale, the number of juveniles reported was 1,300.[10] Assuming that each of the above boys and girls had a set of close friends who were probably in the know about each others' affairs, the total number of youngsters on the edge of being involved with the law was very considerable. It perhaps helped to explain why so many of those met with in the study were so knowledgeable about Trouble.

The youngsters associated fighting, the most obvious of the various types of Trouble, with large formless groups of their contemporaries.[11] They knew a good deal about these gangs and said repeatedly that they were no new phenomena, instancing older brothers now in their mid-twenties who had run around with particular gangs when adolescent. Some of the groups were so loosely structured that they hardly merited the term 'gang'. The Drumchapel 'Bucks' were said to number about 300 youngsters if hangers-on and girl friends, 'Baby' and 'Lady Bucks', were included. A gang's five or six key individuals, young fellows in their late teens and early twenties, were described as louts and deadbeats, 'right bampots'. These key boys often had a local reputation, going back for years, of being children who had never been able to keep a friend and whose behaviour had always been unpredictable and senseless. They were feared as ready to do *anything* to gain an immediate satisfaction and their private ends. A boy who

[9] op. cit. *Report of the Chief Constable of the City of Glasgow.*
[10] *Report of the Chief Constable of Lothians and Peebles Constabulary. 1964.*
[11] cf. *The Ploughboy.* Parker. Hutchinson, 1965.

felt like a brawl could be certain of getting it if he tagged onto them for the night. The one or two young fellows of this kind with whom the team had just a little contact seemed aware of and fatalistic about what the future held for them. They needed the gang much more than the gang members depended on them. Most boys grew out of the gang stage but these 'hard men' stayed on in it. The gangs had a geographical basis. Someone with time to spare could conceivably map their territories from the many tracks—scribbles on bus shelters, hoardings, field gates—they leave behind them. Often enough, they reveal the writers' low educational level. Trouble from gangs was always, of course, ascribed by the youngsters to those from other gangs. Glasgow boys who may or may not have been members of a gang invaded dances as far afield as Bathgate. Armadale complained of the rowdy groups from other West Lothian towns who descended on their own dances. If a gang wanted to pick a fight they chose a place where young people normally congregate. Any dance-hall, with its competition for girls and with many of the company at least slightly loaded, provided a suitable setting. A case in point was the fighting that was a regular feature of Drumchapel's single commercial dance-hall. In general fights were said to be based on a group attack. A minor annoyance was as likely to spark things off as a genuine grudge. The gangs were said to have had their own codes. If you acquired a girl friend you could legitimately drop out. No rules were observed as to clean fighting, 'It's them or you.'

Three points stood out in the youngsters' reactions to gangs and to Trouble in general. They had a genuine fear of physical assault, reflecting an apprehension that appears to be more a feature of working than middle-class society. Many of the boys were convinced that it was dangerous to go about on one's own in certain areas at certain hours and used the plea 'You are never safe' to justify carrying the bicycle chain or knife which, to quote one example, had been sharpened up in the school workshop. Secondly they were very conscious that the bad behaviour of a minority gave their whole age group and district a bad name. This they strongly resented. Thirdly they criticised the popular press as exacerbating matters by blowing up small incidents and by giving the Trouble-makers just the limelight they relished.

Juvenile delinquency is a subject quite outside the competence of those connected with this study and the following comments are plainly very unsophisticated. It was noted that the boys themselves continually made the point that prevention should begin at an earlier age than adolescence. The way in which boys of 16 and 17 referred to the leisure-time needs of those aged 10-12 suggested that the speakers had in mind what they themselves had needed, and failed to find, a few years earlier. They also gave the impression that much, perhaps most, of the fights had no more serious motive than to try to liven things up a bit. Of Drumchapel they said that the place was dead, and that after the week-end, which took most of their money, they had absolutely nothing to do. Compared with the only too well-known routines of home, job and after-work hours, a fight at least offered a possibility of the unfamiliar. Certain ones regarded fighting much as the boys from a 'superior' background looked on rock-climbing or anything that offered risk. 'You go to such-and-such a place *for* the fights' was a comment that explained the complaint of one of the younger boys about 'some old people who go out and call the police just when things are getting interesting'. Once involved in a brawl you cannot turn back even if, as another youngster admitted, you sometimes wished the police would come sooner so that you could clear out. These near artless attitudes recalled the original links between playing and fighting.[12] It was a more innocuous approach than that of the youngsters who were on the lookout for kicks regardless of the ill-consequences to other people. Another set of Trouble-markers were thought to be those whose personalities, according to the psychologists, cannot fulfil themselves without the stimulus of situations which are physically violent. Boys who, so to speak, need fighting, might perhaps find a substitute in some of the tougher types of recreation. The difficulty is that their introduction to such interests mostly presupposes their joining an organised group. And these youngsters are among those who erect their own barriers against joining any formal group. Finally there were the real core of serious Trouble-makers, the 'hard men' and the 'bampots' referred to earlier. In their case Trouble appeared to be associated with psychological disturb-

[12] *Pleg* (Greek) 'a blow': *pleg* (Anglo-Saxon) 'game, sport, usually a skirmish, fight'.

ance which, it was noted, had been spotted way back by their contemporaries. It is a fair guess that their teachers, too, had found them difficult children and that local youth organisations had seen something of, but failed to hold them. In this connection it might be useful to analyse the lapsed membership lists (age 10-12) of the organisations of a locality and to keep an unofficial eye on these particular youngsters for the next five years or so.

In getting at the boys' and girls' own views on Trouble a certain amount of information was picked up on their attitudes to the police. The youngsters thought them necessary, less effective in dealing with Trouble than they should be, held them in scant respect, and made many allegations of injustice. Even the obviously law-abiding had little positive to say in their favour. Typical comment was that 'the police think the clothes we wear are a cause of breaking the law', that 'you get booked for standing at your own close', that 'they are all out to do you' and that 'if you have a weapon they kick your head in'. They fairly often reported cases of near brutality, though the incident had not often happened to themselves. A boy, for example, told of a friend who was 'kicked in the stomach and then kept in for three days'. Two examples of the image of the police which emerged in discussion groups for boys of 17 and 18, one group from Glasgow, the other from Midlothian read as follows:

The group feel the police have no interest in the problems of the young. They are too eager for promotion—sneaky—want glory. Young policemen want to use their authority too much. The police feel that the adolescents are no good. The group felt that the law is against them, always moving them on. They go back to the cafe. Feel it is a vicious circle, with the teenagers in the middle. A young boy who has been in trouble is hounded by the police.

The second group considered that

The police aren't able to do much about it (Trouble). They will arrest you if walking through Bearsden late at night but will let others off with murder in Clydebank and Drumchapel. Cafe-owners in Bearsden will not let you in if you are wearing a leather jacket. Police and others never tackle the real trouble-makers—they watch 40 or so Bucks attacking one or two others and do nothing. They treat ordinary, harmless people like 'dirt' with sarcastic remarks, while insisting on respect from you. (One or two of the boys had been arrested for forming part of a disorderly crowd though they deny this and say they were causing no trouble at all.) There was also talk of corruption and 'backhanders' in the police, though they admitted that policemen had good and bad in their number like any other group.

Both police and adolescents made the point that Trouble would be tackled more effectively if only they knew each other better as persons. The technique by which large numbers of police are drafted into an area to forestall Trouble by breaking up groups may effect a temporary stop but as far as Drumchapel was concerned it increased the boys' and girls' belief that the police were basically hostile and unjust. No comment was collected on the youngsters' reactions to Glasgow's system for minor offences of bringing the boy and his parents before a uniformed Chief Superintendent instead of into court. Two small reactions to the police on the part of Drumchapel adults, as distinct from adolescents, were as follows. The police noted that adults were more ready to call them in than used to be the case; and the parents urged that the police should inform them as quickly as possible if a child of theirs was involved. While part of the youngsters' comment was obviously ill-informed, a good deal appeared to be legitimate insofar as justice was not seen to be done. None of it took account of the tremendous problems that face the Glasgow police due to shortage of man power.

When thinking over what these adolescents of the 1960's had to say about Trouble it may be useful to refer to some of the more obvious changes noted by the writer as regards today's youngsters and those with whom she was in contact before the war. The first difference is that today's boys and girls seem so much more robust physically, look older for their age, and dress and speak far better than did their predecessors. One rarely comes across the stunted, peaky-faced, very illiterate and unvocal youngster who was almost the typical factory girl of the 1930's. At that time, when so many adolescents were obviously deprived as regards their material and educational needs, a good deal of allowance was made not only for uncouthness but for positive misbehaviour. It was half expected. The second difference is that today's youngsters are literally so much more in the public eye than was the case formerly. They comprise a larger proportion of the population, their distinctive gear and speech singles them out, and they have far more economic importance as consumers and as news mass media value. The adolescents of the 1930's obviously contributed their quota of Trouble but their misdemeanours were not continually under the magnifying glass as is the case today. Thirdly, today's adolescents seem more conscious than were their predecessors that society tends to disparage those who do less well at school and who have to settle for the duller and less esteemed job. For certain ones the obvious answer is to kick back in a round-the-clock hostility to things in general, or in deliberate and organised outbreaks. Even today, when the lot of the ordinary youngster has improved so markedly, physical force (the misuse of which constituted much of the Trouble met with in this study) is one of the few tools possessed by certain of these boys and girls.

Chapter VII

CONCLUSIONS

This study, a description and attempted evaluation of young people's leisure-time interests, was based on about two and a half years' consultation with and observation of the 15-19 population of three areas in Central Scotland. The first of these, Dennistoun, is in old Glasgow; the second, Drumchapel, in new Glasgow; and the third is the small West Lothian town of Armadale. Most of the facts about the boys' and girls' use of their free hours came from interviews with a sample of 600 held in the winter of 1964. Another 2,400 or so provided information on the why rather than the how of their leisure. Again all were aged 15-19 but in this case their homes were located in various parts of Glasgow and its contiguous burghs, or, in the case of Armadale, in a somewhat wider area than the town itself. To obtain these views, contact was made with groups of young people. They were located through schools and colleges, churches, firms, social work agencies, youth organisations, etc. One type of information on what the youngsters' thought came from small informal discussion groups, another from what they had to say in written comment. Additional information was derived from two years sustained contact with some 40 boys and girls—the Leavers—between their 15th and 17th birthdays.

Several matters need to be held in mind about the nature of the above material. The study related solely to the 15-19 age group and in the main to three localities only. It was not an investigation into the needs of Scottish youth, nor into the Youth Service of Glasgow and West Lothian. Thus any suggestions for action contained in this report may be applicable only to the area in question though, as said earlier, the three areas were believed to have numerous counterparts. Secondly, the bulk of the information on what the youngsters *thought* came from boys and girls aged 17 and under, not from those in their later teens. Even in the sample interviews which dealt with facts, not views, rather less than 2 in 3 were under $17\frac{1}{2}$, while the

Leavers, an important source of information, were all under 17. Another point to note is that there were two Drumchapel youngsters in the sample for one in Dennistoun and for one in Armadale. Although statistically correct this meant that throughout the study more contact was made with Drumchapel than with the other two areas. Thus the report probably over-emphasises the situation as seen in a new housing estate.

FIG. 11. Club dancing class, Dennistoun

Thirdly, the categories devised for the ways in which the youngsters used their spare hours were arbitrary ones. The major division, leisure spent at home or away from it, was an obvious one, but the subdivisions within the latter tended to overlap. It was not always possible to distinguish the commercially provided type of leisure which mostly attracts large numbers (Leisure II) from the so-styled self-run activities (Leisure I). The third type, leisure which necessitated membership of a formal group, was relatively clear-cut.

The great majority of the sample boys and girls came from working-class homes and thus inherited working-class traditions as to how leisure should be used. Three in four had a father in manual work and about five in six lived in a council house. Their families tended to be large ones. As many as one in three of these youngsters had six or more persons living in their home. A larger than average and probably poorer than average family may well have restricted and clouded the childhood of certain ones. Broken homes were not infrequent. As many as one in nine of these boys and girls had no father in their home and half that number no mother, with all that this can imply.

The boys' and girls' background was reflected in their education. Rather less than half had had no more advanced schooling than that afforded by a junior secondary school, nine in ten had left at the minimum age, and about two in five had received no further education since leaving. Only one in ten, and nearly all of them boys, were still getting any formal education through day release. In other words, the education of the great majority of this sample of the 15-19 population in three 'typical' areas was a limited one. It will be shown later that this was believed to be highly relevant to the way in which they used their free time. The following points were noted. Those still in full-time education or getting day release had practical advantages in the way of sports facilities, school and college clubs, etc., and they were also subjected to some pressure about using their leisure constructively. This suggests that in general the provision for young people's leisure ought to concentrate on those whose contact with formal education has ceased. Secondly, too heavy a load of evening classes, especially when they involved travel, might give the youngster an unduly hard day. Apart from the physical strain, the boy literally had not the time in which to learn to make choices and experiments in the use of his leisure. One could foresee some of these overdriven youngsters growing up into dullish adults. Campaigners for day release, as opposed to evening classes, could take more advantage of parents' attitudes. As consulted in this study, parents almost universally favoured it. Thirdly, any provision for leisure should trade on the long light evenings between May and September when evening classes are finished. One particular batch of youngsters, those who leave school at Easter, ought to be caught up at once into some kind of leisure-time activity which would encourage them to keep on with whatever they had shown pleasure in at school.

The adolescents were very much a group of young wage-earners. Only one in six was still a school child or, in a tiny number of cases, a student. About a third of the boys and perhaps half of the girls were believed to be in the type of job that gave relatively little training or prospect of advancement. On the other hand, half the boys were apprentices or getting a professional training, but this encouraging figure had no parallel for the girls. A surprisingly small number had chopped and changed their jobs excessively. Both earnings and spending money were less high than is generally assumed to be the case for this age group. Rather less than half had a take-home pay of £3 to under £5. In the younger group over half had less than £1 a week spending money, and in the older one, more than half had under £3. Actual wages were, of course, often supplemented by overtime, Saturday morning work, bonuses, etc. These was some evidence that the youngster so to speak slipped into overtime less for the extra money than because he had so limited a conception of how to enjoy free time. In two of the areas, Drumchapel and Armadale, there was less free time available than in Dennistoun, partly because of the time involved in getting to work and partly because most forms of commercial leisure necessitated additional travelling and fares. A final point noted was that shift work, unusual opening hours (e.g. for shop employees) and an annual winter holiday were beginning to provide leisure at unfamiliar times and seasons.

Leisure spent at home

One point which came out strongly in this study of adolescents' leisure was how often home and family still exerted a very considerable influence although the majority were now wage earners. It was interesting to find how much of their free time they in fact spent at home. Most homes were cosy, with a bright fire and comfortable chairs and these creature comforts doubtless exerted their pull even on the foot-loose adolescent. From about 6 o'clock onwards there was a marked sense of relaxation in most homes. Few people seemed to be doing anything more definite than looking at the telly or just chatting. The most common of the youngsters' home-based interests was pop. It demands the minimum of physical effort, requires no space or privacy, is fed daily by the mass media and is likely to be an interest shared with the rest of the family. Pop and the telly would seem to be the obvious starting points from which to try to extend the range of interests which can be pursued at home.

How much did the boys and girls rely on reading as a way of using their free time? In a house with only one living-room their reading had to contend with practical hindrances and a good deal of it was probably done in bed. The youngsters were also handicapped by the absence of books, as distinct from magazines, in their homes. A couple of book shelves built into the council house of the future might be money well spent merely if it jogged some eyes into seeing books as an attractive bit of furniture. If more books were on tap the youngster might come to regard reading as one of the *easy* ways of beguiling an evening at home. Could the public library service experiment with a mobile book van aimed at the adolescent worker and therefore operating at night and at the week-end? Useful things like dictionaries, timetables and local maps should be prominently displayed, and illustrated books on hobbies, sport, space exploration, pets, and the do-it-yourself world. A few paperbacks and magazines of slightly better standard than that to which the adolescent is accustomed might be on sale in addition to the books on loan. The librarian would need to be familiar with the general tastes of the local youngsters and on any subject in which the local secondary schools take a special interest. A couple of voluntary helpers attached to the van (could the Hospital Library Service advise here?) might ease staffing problems and would provide that personal touch which, as all the evidence suggested, is essential in the job of awakening and sustaining a new interest. Another experiment connected with reading might be geared to the workshops and hobby and travel centres referred to below. The youngster who has not got to the stage of reading for enjoyment might begin to handle books if he saw them of immediate use in any practical work on which he was engaged. The specialist consultants at these workshops would point out which book and what part of it might be handy. Quite a small number of books, thirty or so, would be sufficient to start with. Too much choice confuses the non-reader. The books would include flight and motor manuals, model-making books, and those connnected with cooking and crafts. In the case of travel centres, there would be maps, atlases and timetables. Another possible setting for encouraging reading is the youngster's place of work. The adolescents of this study obtained a good deal of their reading matter by swapping magazines and paperbacks with workmates. They often had odd minutes in hand during their working hours and welcomed anything new to look at and talk about. A study of how the adolescent employees of a particular firm or shop spend the dinner hour might show whether some simple book-lending service in this setting would be acceptable.

Many of the other home-based interests were connected with feminine skills like knitting and dressmaking, cooking, and looking after the small children at home. Mechanical skills such as car and motorbike maintenance were another set of interests and there was a certain amount of drawing and painting. One of the questions at the interview, 'Was there anything that you did at school you would still like to do?' revealed a surprising number who said 'Art'. The youngsters in question tended to be shy and sometimes lonely individuals, and since the skills required in imaginative work are different from those needed for the three R's, they had not necessarily been much good at school work. Thus they sheered off anything like an evening class and struggled on alone maybe with a 'painting by numbers' kit. Then, through lack of stimulus, they dropped it all.

Since it was not so much technical help which was needed with these home-based hobbies as encouragement to plod on with them, an experiment on the following lines might be worth trying. As regards the domestic and the mechanical skills and in the case of Art could the Education Authority provide a consultant to operate actually *in one of the youngsters' homes*, but advising both the youngster of that home and a group of 4 or 5 friends whom he had collected? This service would be for a short period only, perhaps six weeks in all. The consultant would not require a fee but the group would have to devise its own methods for compensating the home at which they met. The adult might cope with perhaps three such groups in a night, always bearing in mind the possibility of eventually recruiting a few of the youngsters into an ordinary evening class. There are obvious problems connected with such a scheme, including the difficulty of transporting and storing equipment, but it might perhaps be work with which a retired teacher would experiment. Another possible method of encouraging home-based interests, especially those which involve rough, dirty and large-scale paraphernalia, would be for the Authority to instal a small and very simple workshop providing not much more than cupboard space, good lighting and solid working surfaces. This shed could be erected on the open ground which lies behind most of the modern tenements and which, with synthetic, quick-drying materials and modern washing techniques is now largely under-used. A workshop of this kind might be let, at a modest rent, to the tenants of a particular group of houses. All ages would be allowed to use it and one would hope that youngsters would pick up skills from adults. A simple and very local facility of this nature might be linked with a larger workshop-cum-studio for the adolescents of a wider area. This more elaborate set up would provide working space and basic equipment to be supplemented by the youngster's own tools. It would make for a workmanlike atmosphere and be free of the inevitable distractions of the ordinary youth group. The services of a craftsman-adviser-and-workshop-keeper would be available but he would do no class teaching. Users would pay for the facilities on an *ad hoc* basis and there would be no question of membership. If too many problems—cost, vandalism, caretaking, etc.—are thought to be associated with such a workshop, could a room at a school be allocated and equipped for this type of use? As regards the skills catered for, one workshop might be a place for practising cooking and home-making. Another could be based on car and motorbike maintenance and also meet the common request for driving lessons. A workshop for art and crafts could perhaps be extended to include activities connected with music, dramatics, films and radio.[1] There is the strongest argument for more attention to be paid to the Arts. They have such therapeutic power and are such nourishers of the imagination that to practise them in any form would help dissipate the dullness that characterised the leisure of many of the boys and girls. It might be particularly useful in the case of some of those who turned to Trouble as one way of adding a bit of colour to life. One recalls a comment that Wordsworth made to the young Scot, John Wilson. 'The appropriate calling of youth', wrote Wordsworth, 'is not to analyse . . . but to accumulate in genial confidence: its instinct, its glory is to live, to admire, to feel, and to labour.'[2]

Another aspect of leisure included in home-based interests was holidays since many of the boys and girls did not go away from home and also because holiday plans were very much family affairs. Travel was always a good talking point, appealing to nearly every youngster irrespective of his educational level. The writer's own visit to Czechoslovakia caught the imagination of the most unlikely boys and girls. Lapsed members of youth organisations often spoke about any camping or travelling they had done as members as if this was the most worthwhile thing they had gained. One set to whom travel may be particularly important is the girls aged 17 or so who are referred to later (p. 138). These girls from working-class families found it more difficult to leave home, e.g. for their job, than did their brothers. A little more experience of the world through holiday travel would have helped those who wanted to see more of life before they settled down to cope with the business of living away from home between school and marriage. It might be useful to experiment with setting up a Young People's Holiday Information Centre, functioning perhaps one night a week and charging a small fee. The Centre would give up-to-date information about the wealth of unhackneyed and inexpensive opportunities that exist through such organisations as the Holiday Fellowship, the Ramblers' Association, the International Youth Hostels Association, the Co-operative Society and, of course, the Youth Service. Holidays based on Service should be included and any type of commercial

---

[1] For an imaginative large-scale experiment to encourage young people's concern with the Arts see the Midland Arts Centre in Birmingham.
[2] *William Wordsworth. 'The Later Years'*. Moorman. O.U.P., 1965.

holiday that has obvious value for young people. Information on fairly local travel for day and week-end use would be especially helpful. Though the Centre should push for cheap rate fares for worthwhile travel it should definitely not run travel parties, its job being to stimulate youngsters to make their own choices and plans. Globes, atlases, timetables, maps, slides, phrase books and records should be available for browsing over, and there could be the occasional film show and talk. The Centre might also run a savings scheme and encourage the youngster to set aside any lump sum like a bonus for an exciting holiday. Run on the same such lines, a Travel Centre is basically an educational venture and as such should qualify for grant. Or it might be an experiment which would interest one of the Trusts.

Leisure I

The next set of activities, those grouped under Leisure I, had these characteristics. They were pursued away from home, could often be undertaken with just a few companions or even alone, need not be planned ahead, did not involve membership of a formal group, and were relatively cheap. On the whole they gave more opportunity for choice and initiative than did the provision of the mass entertainment world. They might also involve the youngster in an adult's leisure as with the boy who went fishing with his uncle, or the girl who was swept into the social life of her girl friend's older sister. Dismissing for the moment organised sport, the most interesting thing about the figures for Leisure I was that so many of the youngsters did not pursue any of the activities. The two which topped the list were scratch football for the boys and 'visiting' for the girls. This scratch football played an important part in the life of very many of the boys especially with those who did not find it so easy, or did not want to get into a proper team. The places where boys can get this healthy unsupervised play without causing a nuisance to other people are diminishing all the time. The large distant sports ground does not fulfil the same need as the small site near at hand. There is the strongest case for providing plenty of such sites. The girl's intensive visiting also had many assets, not least that it made her friends known to her home.

It is probably fair to say that a larger number of the boys

wanted more facilities for sport, including undercover provision, than those for any other type of leisure. It was not so much training opportunities for those who wanted to excel which they had in mind as the ordinary player's lack of outdoor, all-the-year-round, all-weather, hard-surfaced and floodlit provision. They also wanted more places not too far from home for indoor physical activities. Boys, and to a lesser extent girls, also made many requests for more and modern swimming baths and for the existing ones to be open for longer hours, especially at the week-end. Though the youngsters in general had not many ideas about new sports or indeed about any new types of provision for leisure, they were emphatic that they wanted more of what they did know about. All the above is

FIG. 12. Football

familiar enough to such bodies as the Scottish Council for Physical Recreation, the Sports Council or the Youth Service. It is only referred to here to emphasise what the youngsters themselves said and because sport is so valuable from the health angle, especially now that the young workers' job is becoming increasingly sedentary.

As regards the facilities needed, the following points were noted.

i) In general the provision for physical recreation ought to be more geared to the needs of the whole community, the schools being one among a number of users. Any new provision at a school should be of a kind that other people can benefit from when the school does not require it. At present the dimensions of these children's sports grounds often make them unsuitable for adult use. The existing provision too is insufficiently available for non-school children. Many grounds are of limited value to young workers because the school takes up the maximum use (about 10 hours a week) of any grass pitch. Also the facilities are shut when the school is closed and therefore they are not available on well over a third of the days in the year. Local Authority-provided gyms, swimming baths, community centre halls, etc. are seldom open to young people unless they join a formal group, and they are only available to a formal group if it is prepared to accept one of the Authority's own instructors which tends to give a class-room rather than a club flavour. Most non-school open-air facilities are dead after dark and may not be used on Sundays when so many adolescents are at a loose end.

ii) The imaginative combination of swimming baths with provision for indoor games should be explored. The Swiss Cottage Leisure Centre in London is an example of careful planning which gives the maximum of use.

iii) Limitations imposed by bad weather and shortage of daylight should be met by more extensive facilities for indoor sports, by all-weather surfacing, by warm changing rooms, and by floodlighting. It is shortage of light rather than bad weather which stops hard tennis courts from being used for over half the year. A climate which is often windy and which suffers from driving rain and the occasional 'creeping cauld prosaic fog' needs outstandingly good provision for indoor recreations.

iv) There is a need for plenty of games, in and out of doors, which require only a few players and unelaborate equipment. Suggestions include such well known games as all-the-year-round basketball, volleyball, deck tennis, and tenni-quoits. Why not explore some equivalent of the French *boules* using metal balls and any hard surface? Or what about the old 'Bumble Puppy' played with a captive tennis ball attached to a tall post? For youngsters below adolescent age there is a crying need for tough, unsupervised apparatus which they can use at any time. Could the Local Authority devise some kind of advanced Jungle Gym—a powerful piece of metal equipment which would test the prowess of boys as old as ten to twelve? A 20 ft. × 30 ft. *balansoir* might be useful.

v) Provision of a more elaborate kind includes trampolining, athletics centres, dinghy sailing in lochs, the use of waterways for safe canoeing, and nylon ski slopes. For an area like Drumchapel an outdoor roller skating rink would be valuable, especially if floodlit.

vi) One of the keys to more participation in physical activities by girls is to give them experience of a wide variety of sports while at school and to see that those who enjoyed an activity, as distinct from the few who shone at it, are encouraged to keep on with it *immediately* they leave. As regards the use girls make of public sports grounds, there is a need for adult helpers who will get new players started and give them reassurance. Drumchapel's tennis courts cried out for one or two older people who, by helping on novices and by looking after the social side of the game, would have encouraged many more girls to 'have a go'. Coaching as such would come later.

vii) The setting where sport takes place should be made more attractive. Pavilions are too often of low standard and locked up. Provision for spectators should be improved in terms of shelter, seating and attractive looks. Simple landscaping such as the occasional timber tree at the corner of a large, hard-surface area, would add to the amenities of sports grounds. And incidentally could not some judicious tree planting be done to civilise and give seasonal variety to the forbidding looks of the traditional school playground? A considerable amount of children's leisure is spent there.

Before leaving the various types of recreation covered by Leisure I, two fringe activities should be mentioned. The first is Service—spending a part of one's free time for the benefit of other people. With the increase in leisure and with voluntary work one of the few expanding sources of manpower, there is a good case for enlarging the idea of Service from the traditional one of face-to-face help between kinsfolk and neighbours.[3] A problem here is that this wider concept is often associated with membership of some formal group. And most adolescents do not belong to any such group. Mass media publicity about Service has some value but is unlikely to solve the perennial problem of how to sell an unfamiliar idea to the less able and the less well educated. Perhaps one of the workshops already referred to (p. 108) might be based on Service. It would be a place where needs, particularly those of the locality, were made known and where the youngsters could make their own plans for coping with them. Experience suggests that it is easier to involve girls in the idea of Service than boys since girls like to feel useful. It was a girl who pointed out that when you are helping people you have no time to get into trouble. Boys, especially the older and tougher ones, present more difficulty. Their imagination might be stirred by some rather grandiose scheme that perhaps involved machinery and was obviously a man's job. Could Glasgow boys be interested in a project like the proposed Kelvin Walk? One of its sections might perhaps be the responsibility of the city's youth and named after them. In all this it is worth noting that such organisations as Enterprise Youth and Interscot have come to the conclusion that there is a fund of idealism in today's young people.

The final set of fringe activities covered by Leisure I was the use which the youngsters made of Scotland's incomparable countryside. What was heard and seen of the boys and girls in general, as well as what was learnt about the leisure of the Leavers, did not suggest that they got out much into the country. Membership of the Youth Hostels Association and of cycling and rambling clubs was low. Nor did they do much in the way of self-run camping, pedal and motor cycling expeditions, or car and bus runs into the country. Things like skiing, climbing, canoeing and sailing were mostly associated with the formal groups to which the majority of the adolescents did not belong. Even had larger numbers taken an interest in specific outdoor recreations, there still remains a case for more youngsters to

[3] *Service by Youth.* Report of the Youth Service Development Council. H.M.S.O., 1966.

turn to the countryside for its own sake. One of the keys here is, of course, intelligent observation. The Council for Nature has a Youth Committee and there are local societies for Natural History which might be prepared to start up, in such places as Drumchapel and Armadale, a local group aimed chiefly at the post-school population. Glasgow itself has such a fine hinterland that every effort should be made to open youngsters' eyes to the wealth which lies almost on the city's doorstep. It is also worth emphasising that, whereas most parts of England have now lost or are rapidly losing the old rural way of life in which British culture is rooted, Scotland still retains what is not only of profound interest in itself but also provides a respite from the mounting pace, pressures and trivialities of urbanisation. Nor should one dismiss lightly the unconscious influences which mountain and sea, loch and burn may exert at the impressionable age of adolescence when the senses are unusually keen.

Leisure II

The really big numbers did not show up until certain of the commercially provided types of recreation, Leisure II, were examined. In terms of use the most popular were the cinema, dancing and cafe-going, and in that order. As many as 81% of the sample went regularly to the cinema, 69% to dancing and 51% to a cafe. Neither sex, age nor educational situation made any marked difference. Leisure II also scored over Leisure I in that a higher proportion of the boys and girls took part in a particular activity twice or more times a week.

Pub-going is discussed later (p. 141). The most interesting point about the remaining three activities (ice-skating, spectator sport and ten-pin bowling) was that so few took part. Only 8% went regularly to watch sport, nearly all boys and nearly all to football matches. This low figure presumably reflects the general decline in football attendance, a drop of 12 million at league matches between 1951 and 1962. Skating and bowling attracted only 7% and 3% respectively. Skating has much to commend it. It is healthy, can take place indoors, is a useful alternative to dancing as a meeting place, and is one of the limited number of active recreations which appeals to girls. The managers of three rinks frequented by the youngsters of this study (Glasgow, Falkirk and Paisley) estimate that at least three-quarters of the 5,000-7,000 weekly attenders are adolescents. Though outdoor skating does not meet quite the same needs as the covered ice rink, the possibility of flooding tennis courts might be explored. And incidentally, more facilities for roller skating would be valuable, especially for the younger adolescent. This is inexpensive provision and with seats, coloured lights and perhaps a milk bar, can attract spectators as well as skaters.

Much of the popularity of Leisure II was associated with matters extraneous to the activity itself. For example, the cinema is more readily available than are many other facilities. It gives opportunity for choice as cinemas are plentiful and programmes change frequently. It also meets courting needs since it provides a reasonably comfortable setting where there is no obligation to show prowess or even to have to talk. No attempt was made to examine the cinema's influence as regards the films seen, but it plays so important a social role that it is a definite need for any sizable community, particularly one with a high proportion of young people. If a cinema is not commercially viable for a place like Drumchapel (though Armadale with only a quarter of Drumchapel's population supports one) could the Local Authority provide or subsidise it, perhaps putting the premises to other uses also? Or would some organisation interested in raising cultural levels experiment in a place like Drumchapel with the kind of cinema that shows the occasional non-commercial film?

The extent to which dancing, the next most popular activity, was associated with Trouble strongly suggests that better provision should be made and also that there should be stricter supervision of halls frequented by large numbers of those still in their early teens. The frequency of fights at Drumchapel's small, single, crowded and presumably highly profitable dance hall was evidence of the need for more facilities and tighter control. Any new provision must be stylish enough to attract young adults or it will not get the older adolescents. It might be useful if inexpensive dances could be run for the younger teenager on Saturday afternoons and early evenings, making sure that such dances do not deteriorate into kids' affairs. If sufficiently glamorous-seeming they might hive off some of those most at risk as regards late-night dancing. They might also attract the rather older and quieter adolescent who gets fed up with the fights. Regular examination of the conditions at dances should concentrate on the physical standards (proper cloakroom facilities, lighting, etc.); staffing (how do the bouncers handle the young people?); the extent to which drinking is really controlled; and late night transport arrangements.

Some interesting and rather unexpected evidence from the youngsters themselves strongly supported the view that cafes provide a valuable social function for this age group. Like the pub, the cafe fosters the day-to-day contacts and the sharing of interests that give warmth to a locality. It is a more civilised setting for talk than hanging about the fish shop or just wandering around. As a place where youngsters have an opportunity to size each other up, it is certainly to be preferred to the Main Street monkey parade of pre-war days. The three areas provided useful contrasts as regards provision for cafe-going. Some or other of Dennistoun's numerous cafes were always available and they were never packed out. They were also sufficiently numerous for the youngsters to sort themselves out socially which seemed to lessen the risk of Trouble. The same applied to Armadale where the cafes played an important part in knitting the young people of the town together and in enabling them to enjoy some of their leisure near home. Drumchapel, with four times Armadale's population and a much higher proportion of adolescents, had no commercial cafe apart from one which kept shop hours. The estate's one experience of a cafe available at night, started by a local man and housed in poor premises, was a sorry story. The place was besieged by youngsters, wrecked, never re-started, and no one else has had the temerity to open up. In any case the typical cafe owner looks for old and cheap premises, seldom has the capital to build and certainly not to put up several cafes as is necessary if Drumchapel's history is not to be repeated. When commercial enterprise cannot be induced to go to a large cafe-less area like a housing estate, would the Local Authority step in, bearing in mind that a variety of cafes offers the important element of choice, and that several small are less likely than a single large one to attract Trouble. Apart from seeing that premises are adequate as regards numbers and hygiene, cafe-going would seem to be an aspect of young people's leisure that should be, and indeed is better, left alone.

One small but interesting point connected with the Leisure II activities was the way in which good transport could step up the numbers taking part in a particular activity. The Armadale youngsters had an eight mile bus journey to reach an ice rink, yet the proportion of those who said they went regularly and of those who had been in the last seven days, was more than double that for Dennistoun or Drumchapel where a rink was much more accessible. The key seemed to be the special skaters' buses which not only eased the journey but added to the fun. More use should be made of tempting transport to encourage various types of worthwhile leisure. A second general observation on the Leisure II activities is that their many social assets and the extent to which they are used by adolescents make it highly desirable that they should be properly run and adequate in quantity for local needs. The police, the schools and the Youth Service are three of the obvious watchdogs. It would also be sensible to enlist the interest of the manager and staff of any place frequented by large numbers of adolescents.

Formal groups

The fourth type of leisure examined was that which necessitated membership of any kind of formal group. Compared with the previous ways of using their leisure the formal group played less part in the youngsters' free time than did Leisure I or II. The number of individuals who had taken part in one or more of the Leisure II activities during the last seven days was four times as great as that for those who had been at one or more of the formal groups. Nor did the youngsters use the formal group on a more than once-a-week basis as much as they did with Leisure II. All the evidence—the figures from the sample, the two years contact with the Leavers, and general observation—suggested that the majority of this 15-19 age group—did not use a formal group for their leisure time. The negative figure, that for those who did not belong, was the reliable one since the positive figure ran the risk of overlapping membership. Table 24 showed 61% as not belonging to any group. Neither age nor sex made very much odds nor were area differences really marked. As expected, the bulk of what membership there was applied to organisations within the Youth Service. Dismissing those who belonged to groups other than these, and bearing in mind the possibility of overlapping membership, the order of popularity was youth clubs 14%, uniformed organisations 9%, youth fellowships 7% and Local Authority recreational centres and clubs 6% (Table 24).

An interesting point was the strong link between current educational situation and membership of a formal group[4]. Of those still in full-time education, 41% of the boys and 31% of the girls were non-members, while for those at work the figures had risen to 68% and 65% respectively. It was not possible (for the whole 600 boys and girls) to match past or present educational level with their current use of a formal group, but it seemed highly probable that the two were related. In Dennistoun, where educational level as judged by the proportion of the sample who had stayed on at school voluntarily after 15 was higher than in Armadale, the percentage of non-joiners was lower than in Armadale—57% compared with 67%. Membership of a youth club as such was nearly twice as high in Dennistoun as in Drumchapel or Armadale. Another hint of the link between the youngster's educational level and the use he made of formal groups was that so few of the Leavers, all of whom had left school at the minimum age, belonged to a youth organisation. The availability or otherwise of formal groups bears on membership figures but by and large mere availability did not seem to be all that relevant.

Why did so many of the boys and girls sheer off a formal group? Before commenting it may be useful to have yet another glimpse of some actual non-joiners as described by two 16-year-old writers.

This person lives in my street and his girlfriend lives in the centre of the city. He says there is very little good talent goes to youth clubs and that there is no drink there. My friend is 18 and likes cars and sports so long as it is not too energetic. He has £3 pocket money a week of which £1 goes towards paying up his car. He is independent but gets on well with people. He has a good way with girls and prefers them to youth clubs.

I know of a girl who is not interested in youth organisations, she likes to go to the dancing, not at the youth organisations though. Sometimes she goes to the pictures. I am not very sure why she does not like the youth clubs, but I think it is because she used to go to a youth club but it was always the same crowd that went and so she got fed up and decided to go to the dancing in the town and she now has friends everywhere in all the different dances.

[4] *op. cit.* Ferguson and Cunnison.

'His family does not care for him' was how the third writer described a non-joiner of his acquaintance and went on to say that the boy had loads of money.

No satisfactory explanation exists as to why about two in three adolescents (a figure which remains oddly stable) do not join the groups connected with the Youth Service. As far as the boys and girls of this study were concerned their chief objection centred on what they felt was an over-authoritatian set-up. They complained that they were too much bossed around and that it was the grown-ups' show, not their own. Also they were made to take part in activities whereas what many of them wanted was to use the group as a base for their social life. One typical comment read:

The club should be run by youths so that there would be no elders' opinion given about the teenagers today. If the club was run by teenagers there would be less chance of their revolting and making trouble as most young people do not like being dictated to by other elders outside their own family.

It is a healthy sign that many youngsters who are as old as 15-19 should reject imposed patterns as regards their leisure. They ought to be making choices for themselves and should be given every encouragement to run their groups for themselves. At the same time they must recognise that the experience of older people has some value and that if the group depends on adult finance, then adults will expect some measure of control. One of the answers to the youngsters' criticisms is for the unit to avoid too rigid a set-up and to work through small groups within the total framework. This encourages choice and enables the members to have a considerable amount of say in the group's affairs. At school and in their job both may be out of the question. The quite small group also fosters the possibility of making contacts with other people in width and depth. Once the youngster has begun to tackle this he is freer to turn his attention to activities. The small group technique is especially useful for the less able adolescent. Teachers point out that the junior secondary school child is not just less mature, but lives and learns through his personal relationships and his emotions more than does the senior secondary child. If he is hurt he closes up and stops trying. Group work, however, is more than a question of training in techniques. Its success depends very much on the ratio of adults to members. If the unit has only a handful of older people to perhaps 80 adolescents with the best will in the world it is difficult to avoid the classroom-like flavour to which adolescents are so allergic.

The success of the lively 62 Club at Aberdeen seems to rest partly on the fact that its working groups are mostly quite small—perhaps not more than half a dozen individuals. The popularity of the Drumchapel informal discussion group, which attracted chiefly 'non-joiners', was thought to be largely

FIG. 13. 'Going to the pictures'

due to its intimate character. A typical group involved only seven or eight youngsters. The physical setting, too, a little room (and no other distractions in the building) encouraged the exchange of ideas on things that really mattered to these youngsters. One of the topics which cropped up continually was this vexed question of authority in youth groups. The talkers plainly needed the chance to thrash out with someone that much more mature than themselves what was often a startlingly new conception to them, namely that some limitation of personal freedom is not a matter of knuckling under. It is the price paid for the benefits of belonging to a group.

A second reason why many of the boys and girls sheered off the youth organisations was because they associated them with school. The figures showed that those who had stayed on voluntarily after 15 and who, presumably, had liked school, were relatively ready to join a formal group irrespective of the fact that so many of these groups were school-linked. Those who had left school as soon as possible tended to erect barriers against any group which had any connection with formal education. Distaste for school was widespread. Some had hated it while others considered that it had no relevance to real life. Adolescents are very conscious of their ever vanishing youth and in a way they are betraying themselves if they deliberately hang on to the immediate past which school represents rather than go forward to a more adult stage. Even some of those who were still only 15 or 16 considered the Youth Service puerile and were vaguely derisive of it. As was shown earlier (p. 80) a large number of the groups were, in fact, children's affairs rather than composed of those aged 15 and over. Apprehensions about a group merely because it uses school premises might be countered by trying to get away from school's desk-and-blackboard aura. Easy chairs and small tables can be introduced and could the School Meals Service perhaps help with portable coffee bars? Purpose-built club annexes to schools are of course a much sounder answer. If the Youth Service is to be increasingly linked with formal education, which is the likely pattern, the crux of the matter is that his schools should have left a relatively favourable image on the youngster even if he did not do particularly well at the actual lessons.

The boys' and girls' rejection of the church-linked organisations did not seem to stem from hostility to the Church as such. But they associated church with social class—'the church youth organisations are for snobs'. The comment ran much on the following lines, in this case from a boy of 16.

People who are not in the social class of the elders are given an inferiority complex as if they were not worthy of worshipping because of their social status. The youth club in my Church is too posh. People like myself are made to feel inferior.

They also mistrusted any group if they thought it was being provided as a bait to step up church membership. Certain individuals of course kept clear of certain church groups on sectarian grounds, others because their family had broken with a church. The Church has always taken such a lead in youth work and is plainly doing such an effective and worthwhile job in the Youth Service at the present time that it seems churlish to criticise the church-linked groups. But anyone who has hunted about for a suitable group for a particular youngster to join knows just how the association with a church narrows the choice in what, in any case, is seldom an extensive range. All this in no way decries the special value of the group associated with the Church. Certain of the youngsters strongly preferred such a group. It guaranteed standards. Nor should one minimise the never ending practical problems of the group which has no stable parent body. But if the total membership of youth groups is to be stepped up, the Youth Service must make provision for those youngsters (and their families) who are anti-teacher and anti-church. The situation was particularly evident in Armadale where practically all the groups were either school or church-linked. Any community with a sizable number of adolescents (500 in the 15-19 age range?) probably needs at least one group which has no obvious link with church or school.

The nature of the formal group means it is not likely to be all that available as a way of spending leisure. Most of those in the three areas which were run by the voluntary youth organisations were only open on one evening a week and most of the youngsters who belonged to a group of any kind attended on a once a week basis. On the other hand a noticeable feature in the lives of these young workers was the variety in the times—day, week and year—when they were not at work. A shift job might bring the boy home by three o'clock. Or a girl had a mid-week morning off, instead of Saturday morning. Or her firm now gave a winter as well as a summer holiday. Sunday was dead as regards formal groups except for church ones, the Boys' Brigade and the youth fellowships in particular. Glasgow Local Authority's clubs and centres, any organisations using school premises, and any Authority-provided instructors were not available when the schools were closed. These major services for young people's leisure were therefore not available for over a third of the year. And this included just those periods, the week-end, the New Year and Easter holidays, and the schools' eight summer holiday weeks, when so many of the youngsters, especially the school children, were noticeably at a loose end. The excuse that they were away on holiday was hardly valid. As said earlier, though more than half went away, in most cases it was not for longer than a week. It is obviously very difficult for groups which are staffed largely by voluntary workers to increase their regular nights of opening but they could turn more attention to the odd week-end and to the period covered by the schools' summer holidays. Now that the Youth Service has a modicum of salaried staff there is the strongest case for trying to fit its provision more realistically to the times when young people get their leisure.

One of the functions of the Youth Service is to push the opportunities for worthwhile leisure in general, as well as to recruit for youth groups. Any salesmanship must bear in mind not only the youngster's age but his educational situation, i.e. it should distinguish between those still at school, those who have left but are still getting some part-time education, and the ones who have no contact with the educational world. Full advantage should be taken of any information teachers have on what the boy or girl *enjoyed*. Places where youngsters are employed, even if in small numbers, ought to have an unofficial agent for the Youth Service. It would be an interesting experiment (financed by one of the Trusts?) for the Service to run a mobile van dealing solely with hot news about the relatively local opportunities for leisure, and not confining this to activities connected with the Service itself. The more local the information the better. This means referring to particular streets and using personal names and photographs. Advance publicity on the occasional special event is less effective from the recruitment angle than facts about what is taking place at the moment with the implication that 'You too can take part—tonight if you like, at latest next week'. A leisure telephone service might be tried. 'Are you aged 15-19? Then ring ... for interesting ways of spending your free time this coming week.' Any spot from which food is collected is a natural centre for disseminating news. Dennistoun's corner shops on a Sunday morning are one example, so are Drumchapel's innumerable van shops and Armadale's fish bar when the cinema comes out. This sort of recruitment is unlikely to touch the very shy or those with personality problems. But most of the boys and girls met were normal youngsters and to outward appearances just a little push would have galvanised them into less hackneyed and fundamentally more enjoyable ways of spending their free time.

How did the adults of the three areas regard the Youth Service and youth groups? It was widely held that the purpose of the Service was a negative one—to divert young people, and in particular boys, from Trouble. There was not much conception of the Service as one that makes any positive contribution to the life of the boy or girl. Another mistaken idea was that activities—canoeing, judo, drama, sport—were the be all and end all whereas the deeper value of the Service is that it encourages youngsters to cope with some of the problems in social relationships that harass our ever bigger and ever more anonymous society. Anyone who works with a youth group senses something of what it can offer in this field, and especially in helping the ex-junior secondary school youngster to feel 'I matter.' There was also a need to hammer home to adults that the difference between the Youth Service provision and that of commercial entertainment lies not in the activities, which are often similar, but in the goals.[5] One raking question asked by certain adults who were genuinely concerned with young people's welfare was whether a Youth Service may not be meddling with and coddling a side of the youngster's life where he ought to be making his own choices. 'Don't let anyone else use *your* leisure' was the kind of warning they would give. Unless the group is run on genuinely democratic lines their apprehensions are well founded. A strong argument in

[5] *Girls at Leisure.* Hamer. London Union of Girls' Clubs and Y.W.C.A., 1964.

favour of a Youth Service, and one which was seen repeatedly in this study, was that those who did belong to a group had more opportunities offered to them than had the non-joiners. They got around more, literally and mentally. For example, the non-joiners among the Leavers were continually missing out on opportunities that were being made available to their contemporaries who did belong to some youth group. However simple these opportunities they tended to have a quality about them which was missing in much of what the youngster was getting from the mass entertainment world. It was, for example, the boy or girl Leaver who belonged to a youth group who knew about the new interests and challenges presented by the Duke of Edinburgh's Award. Another of the youth group's assets is that it provides a meeting ground for the generations. The youngsters in the Drumchapel discussion group said how much they valued the chance to talk on equal terms with one or two adults. And would not many older people reciprocate this? For all the failings of the youth group, the typical one has a distinctive, indefinable quality—some combination of camaraderie, honesty and care—that gives it value. Youngster or adult, anyone who is familiar with these groups knows that our society would be the poorer without them.

As regards the Youth Service in general, this study was only concerned with it in so far as the Service is one of many agents which provide for young people's leisure. Another limitation was that whereas the Service caters for an age range of 8-20, the study was confined to that of 15-19. Then, too, the population of the three study areas comprises only a fraction of that covered by the Service as operating in Glasgow and West Lothian. Lastly only about 1 in 3 of the adolescents met with through the sample belonged to a formal group of any kind, while relatively few of the Leavers, a specially reliable source of information, had any contact with a youth group.

What was seen of the work of the voluntary organisations within the Service gave the impression that they were keen and efficient. That they were prepared to do experimental work with the post-school adolescent and with the tougher youngster was particularly noticeable in such an organisation as the Glasgow and West of Scotland Association of Youth Clubs. Those in charge of the organisations appeared to favour the various reappraisals which their headquarters have undertaken in the last few years.[6] The conclusions drawn from this re-examination of aims and methods suggests that the organisations are widening their concept of what they should be doing. They will be helped here by the fact that the Kilbrandon Council has changed its constitution to enable it to become a consultative body for community as well as for youth work. Perhaps the most encouraging feature of the youth organisations, as seen in this study, was their emphasis on training. The writer was impressed by the scale on which training was being provided by the Education Authorities and by the voluntary organisations in Scotland and also by the numbers, over 12,000 people in 1964-5, who were prepared to take courses of sustained training.[7] One important aspect of training, the new course in professional youth work which was started at the Jordanhill College of Education just as this study began, was already making its impact in all three of the study areas before the enquiry was finished. An influx of professionals will help to canalise what has always been one of the weaknesses of youth work, viz. a tendency to 'shapeless enthusiasm'. The new standing of the professionally trained leader with a recognised salary scale will also improve the prestige of the Service and therefore of recruitment to it. The extent to which it is voluntary workers who continue to run the formal group type of provision for young people's leisure, is shown in the figures for Scotland as a whole. In 1964/5 the number of full-time paid youth workers for Scotland was 246, of whom 65 were employed by Education Authorities. The 12,700 units of the 31 main types of youth organisation had some 434,000 members, of whom 197,000 were between the ages of 12 and 21. Of the local leaders connected with these units, some 36,000 of the 37,000 concerned were voluntary workers, and of the 1,566 headquarters and field staff, 1,467 were unpaid. However numerically important, willing and efficient these voluntary workers may be, it is out of the question for them to run more than a fraction of the groups which, open pretty well

---

[6] *The Haynes Committee Report*. The Boys' Brigade, 1964; *The Advance Party Report '66*. The Boy Scouts Association, 1966; '*Tomorrow's Guide*'. Report of the Working Party 1964-1966. The Girl Guides Association, 1966; *Reaching the Teenager*. The Methodist Association of Youth Clubs.

[7] *Progressive Joint Training of Part-time Youth Leaders*. Standing Consultative Council on Youth and Community Service, 1966.

throughout the day, week and year, are really needed if changing patterns of leisure are to be catered for and a much larger proportion of youngsters profit by all that a strong Youth Service can offer.

Lack of full-time staff was a weakness noted in all three of the study areas. Another was the shortage of women staff, a disability to both boy and girl members. The impermanence of staff and of units was another disturbing matter, difficult to avoid but nearly always a let down to the youngster. The stabilising virtues of a sustained group and of sustained relationships cannot be over-emphasised at this stage when so much else in the adolescent's life is changing. Another weakness of the voluntary organisations, again relating to the shortage of full-time staff, was their lack of ability to supply precise information on their membership in relation to its age, sex, educational background and the volume of attendance. Such material is essential for planning new work. In any case, solid figures strengthen the likelihood of grant aid. One problem noted as regards the voluntary side of the Service concerned the Glasgow Standing Conference of Voluntary Youth Organisations. A vigorous local Conference is a valuable agent in spotlighting deficiencies in the Service and in making economical use of what, nearly always, are limited resources. If the efficiency of Glasgow's Standing Conference is restricted primarily because of lack of funds, should the Authority not give it more financial help?

The writer was impressed by the vigorous, imaginative and constructive lead the Scottish Education Department takes in the Service at all its levels, and by its first-hand knowledge of individual units and their personnel up and down the country. A typical example of its down-to-earth appraisal of the needs and tastes of young people is shown in its lively quarterly publication, *Scottish Youth News*.

Incidental contacts with that branch of the Youth Service which operates in Armadale suggested that it was satisfactory as far as the existing youth groups were concerned. Regular and personal consultation took place between them and the staff of the Service. The case for more provision for outdoor sport and for one 'open' club for a local population of 8,000 are referred to elsewhere (pp. 30, 123).

Some indication of the nature and scale of the Service in

Glasgow is given in the figures shown in Appendix B. At the time this study was finishing two large youth centres on new housing estates were about to be opened and two others were to be ready in 1967. These centres will have large games halls attached to them. The cost, as given in the estimates for 1965/6, will be £250,000. Another new provision is the youth wings (club, committee and leader's rooms, cafe, etc.) which are to be included in all new secondary schools. By 1970 twenty-six such wings should be in use. In the 1965/6 estimates the cost for each youth wing is £18,000. At certain schools where the Authority runs youth clubs and evening centres, experiment is now being made in setting aside one room during the evening for social purposes. New premises will give the opportunity to introduce staff of the tutor/leader or youth/tutor type. All these developments are, of course, in line with the movement to bridge the gap between the schools and the Youth Service. As a recent book points out, this gulf has been referred to in every official report on adolescents for the last 20 years.[8]

The above very considerable advances to be made in the city's Youth Service were not public knowledge at the time when the field work of this study was taking place. This may help to explain why one of the current themes encountered during the study was criticism of the Authority's work as regards its Youth Service. The considered views of many of the adults met with—and not only people who were connected with the voluntary organisations but teachers, ministers, social workers, etc.—turned on four main issues. The first was that the 60-odd (recreational) centres and clubs run by the Authority for the 14-19 age group, in fact attracted chiefly those aged under 15, i.e. school children. Though welcoming the older adolescent, the set-up was not such as to bring in any conciderable number of them. Indirect criticism on similar grounds was recorded from many of the youngsters themselves. They dismissed the Authority's provision as 'kid's affairs'. The adult critics also pointed out that, as any youth leader knows, it is easier to hold the youngster who is at school than the older and more sophisticated one who is in a job and has more money to burn. Another aspect of the Service, Glasgow's admirable provision of cruises and exchange visits with other countries,

[8] *Young People in Society*. Evans. Blackwell, 1966.

was criticised as being taken up chiefly by those still in full time education, not by the young worker who forms the bulk of the 16-19 group and so often needs just this kind of eye-opener. In 1966 about two-thirds of the 600-odd youngsters who went abroad were still in full-time education and thus already getting all the advantages that school or college confers. Secondly, it was questioned whether the Authority was up to date in its approach to group work.[9] Did it take serious account of the adolescent's need to acquire skill in personal relationships, or was it almost entirely concerned with providing activities through a modified form of class teaching? Neglect of modern group work techniques was said to be reflected in the nature of the Authority's training courses and in the qualifications it required of those staffing its own units and of those it provided for the voluntary organisations.

As the Authority was not itself catering for any considerable number of the 15-19 age group it was held that it ought to give more adequate support to those of the voluntary organisations which were working with the older and more demanding adolescents. The estimates of expenditure for the financial year 1965/6 threw some light on this point. They included £300,000 for direct provision by the Authority, and almost £100,000 for its assistance to youth organisations under the control of the voluntary bodies (salaries, grants, use of school premises). The figures in Appendix B (Assistance given by Authority for the Financial Year 1964-5) show that though it spent nearly £31,000 on accommodation for voluntary organisations using its own premises and nearly £21,000 on staff for them, it did not give them any very considerable support in other ways. Only 26 of the non-Authority units received grants (£6,000 in all) towards staff employed directly by themselves, and only 45 units had help (£15,000) towards the rent or maintenance of their premises. It is probably typical of those engaged in youth work that, as met with in this study, they made little reference to personal financial reward. It was only the odd, voluntary helper who, on occasion, drew a wry comparison between his own slogging evening with a group of roisterers in their mid-teens, and that of the instructor at one of the Authority's groups where the members were mostly still at school and for which a two-hour session earned a fee of 53/-

[9] *Working with Groups.* Matthews. University of London Press, 1966.

A fourth and less tangible matter was the relationship between the voluntary and statutory sides of the Service. Though this had improved, the Authority was criticised for not taking a strong enough lead in establishing the One Service which is so continually stressed by, for example, the Chairman of the Standing Consultative Council on Youth and Community Service. There was said to be not enough contact between the individual voluntary organisation and the Authority's staff, although easy communication, based on first-hand and up-to-date knowledge of each other's work in the field, is essential in a Service so dependent on volunteers and with units so heterogeneous in character. Even the 'creative quarrel' which, often enough, raises standards was said to be missing. As far as the Authority is concerned, the crux of many of the above matters would appear to be staffing. Two Youth Service officers, the position at the time of the study, is hopelessly inadequate for a Service to some 90,000 boys and girls of 15-19, quite apart from its obligations to the younger age groups.

As said before, the above comments were made before the very considerable developments about to take place in the Service were public knowledge. Nor did the critics take account of Glasgow's heavy financial commitments as regards housing and education, nor of its acute problems over teacher shortage. Compared with these, the leisure-time needs of a Drumchapel apprentice or a girl checker-out in a Dennistoun supermarket sound small beer. On the other hand, when there are unavoidable deficiencies in the provision for formal education, it is legitimate to argue that this strengthens the case for a very efficient Youth Service. So huge and vital a city as Glasgow deserves an outstandingly good Service. The fact that the criticism was widespread suggests that it would be sound for the Authority to clarify certain of the above matters, particularly as to just what youngsters make use of its own faciliites. Age, sex, educational background and type of job is the kind of basic information needed, together with some indication of the volume of attendance made by the individual boy or girl.

The Local Authority is, of course, the fountainhead for financial provision for leisure in a far wider field than that of the Youth Service. *A Policy for the Arts* indicates how its powers have grown since the Physical Training and Recreation Act of 1937.

Local Authorities depend for authority to incur expenditure mainly, but not entirely, on Section 132 of the Local Government Act 1948. This permits them to spend the product of a sixpenny rate on entertainment in all its forms. They can also spend whatever income they receive from entertainment. There is a similar provision for Scotland.[10]

The 1937 Act and the additional legislation made since then means that most of the provision that youth workers are likely to think desirable could probably be put into effect. As things are, most Authorities spend much less than is permitted. It cannot be over-emphasised that the legislation does more than empower—it lays a duty on the Authority to meet recreational needs.

The above general comment may be given more reality by quoting what certain of the Glasgow youngsters, all aged 16-19 and all at school, had to say about the facilities for leisure in their own localities. They were replying to the question, 'If

FIG. 14. Nowhere to go

[10] *A Policy for the Arts—the First Steps*, H.M.S.O. Cmnd. 2601.

the Corporation consulted you on how to spend £10,000 for teenagers in your own part of the city, what would you advise them?'

I would advise them to build a youth organisation, because many teenagers have very few facilities in which to spend their spare time, and the lack of clubs for boys causes a greater rate in vandalism. (*Toryglen*)

I would advise the Corporation to provide adequate leisure facilities for the *Croftfoot* District in order to put an end to the aimless wanderings of so many of the teenagers in the aforesaid area.

With £10,000 I would like to see a new teenagers club and sports centre started to combat the growth, which is quite alarming, of teenage gangs in the district. The district mentioned is the *N.W. Glasgow*.

I would advise them to spend the money on sports facilities for the district of *Castlemilk*. Although this area contains a few tennis courts (three) and four football grounds this number is well below the requirements for an area which ranks as one of the largest Housing schemes in Britain. I would also advise them to spend part of the money on entertainment such as dancing, bowling (indoor) and Cinemas. Vast as this area may be it does not contain one of the above items for the teenagers entertainment.

My district is *Langside*. I would advise the Corporation to improve entertainment facilities for the young since a growing number of Cinemas in our area have been closing down. I think boredom is the biggest problem of youth and contrary to common opinion we do not have more money than we know what to do with.

I would suggest a club or some other form of recreation for these teenagers who run about in gangs terrorising the people in *Maryhill*. This is just one place.

Before concluding this section it may be useful to reiterate what was said earlier (p. 25) about the special needs of a new housing estate such as Drumchapel, even though the problems associated with large estates are common knowledge. One of the chief causes of malaise stems from the distorted age structure of the population. An abnormally high proportion of young people means that the place has to put up with a tremendous amount of wear and tear in every sense. *Extra* Services are needed to stop the estate's physical appearance from deteriorating and to support the efforts of the many residents who, as their gardens prove, do care about the looks of their part of the city. Would it be too bizarre to suggest that there is now a case for a service vaguely parallel to that of the first Health Visitors? Although without legal powers they nevertheless did a great deal in the early part of the century to begin to pull up standards of child and home care. The personnel of any such experimental service in estate care would include experts on fencing, playground designers, and landscape gardeners, as well, of course, as advisers on small-scale gardening. It is very difficult to see how any dent can be made in another of Drumchapel's problems, the over-uniformity of its economic and social structure. So long as mobility is frozen through restrictions on house buying and private building, the estate is likely to remain a working-class enclave, yet another example of what Professor Merritt calls 'a two nation society based on tenure of occupation'.[11] Another disability is the lack of day-to-day opportunities to enlarge oneself that derive from casual contacts. Any new community needs all sorts of mixing bowls, but even after 10 years Drumchapel still lacks corner shops, cafes, milk bars, pubs, hotels, billiard halls, sports pavilions—informal meeting places large and small. This is not to disparage the action which has already been taken. The new community centre is a tremendous asset, as will be the new swimming baths and the new youth centre. But for a population of 40,000 they are only a drop in the bucket. There is also a need for more experiment as regards formal groups and for implementing some of the suggestions outlined in the Kilbrandon Council's 'Interim Report of Linkage Committee'.[12] As regards provision for young people in general, it might be sounder in a new locality like Drumchapel to work on facilities for the community as a whole rather than concentrating over-much on separate ones for adolescents.

Certain of the boys and girls were noticeably 'at risk' as regards their leisure. Fate had probably already stacked the cards against those with low I.Q.s and those who had suffered serious social disabilities as children. The occasional near-waif was still to be found, like the 15-year-old girl encountered at mid-afternoon in a squalid, broken-windowed, fireless home minding the neighbour's children. Motherless since she was seven, this child already had a couple of jobs behind her and

[11] 'Are Council Estates today's Ghettos?' Merritt. *The Times*, December 11, 1965.
[12] *Interim Report of Linkage Committee*. Standing Consultative Council on Youth and Community Service, 1965.

was now unemployed. Such youngsters plainly required general care before anything effective could be done about their leisure.[13] Others at risk tended to come from unusually large families, from housholds where one parent was incapacitated, perhaps an invalid or an alcoholic, or from incomplete homes. Motherless brothers, or the girl brought up by her grandmother were among those who often spent an unusually large proportion of their free time out of their home. The boy's or girl's job was another matter which might indicate risk, as with those who had a chequered history of job changes, or the dozen or so who, even in this sample of 600, had never had a job. Or their work might be very binding like that of the cafe-owner's daughter who worked long and irregular hours. Another set of youngsters who had a very circumscribed leisure were the isolates, unoffending creatures who could not name a single friend. For example, there was the girl who, to quote an interviewer, was,

introspective and not good at expressing herself. She feels clumsy and inadequate and could be in some danger of becoming a permanent recluse ... fails to come to grips with the adjustments demanded in the transition from childhood to adulthood. She is a serious nail-biter and exhibits a constant state of unease and jerkiness which only settles when she becomes immersed in television. She does not get out nearly enough.

Physique, clothes and speech were other matters which sometimes helped to identify those at risk. Certain of the boys and girls looked and sounded less robust and less competent than their contemporaries. On the whole these 'poor doers' (in the farmer's sense) were ex-junior secondary school youngsters. Apart from their other handicaps, their educational level would probably hamper their future both as regards work and play.[14] All told, a surprising number of the boys and girls did not conform to the popular image of the cocksure, 'with it' adolescent. It is difficult to see how the Youth Service, as operating now, could have helped many of the above youngsters, bearing in mind that they tended to be individuals who had not acquired the social skills which are needed to take advantage of a youth organisation. Once spotted, perhaps through their

---

[13] *Children and Young Persons.* Scotland. H.M.S.O. Cmnd. 2306. 1964.
[14] cf. 'The Trend of Class Differentials in Educational Opportunity in England and Wales'. Little and Westergaard. *The British Journal of Sociology*, Vol. XV No. 4, December 1964.

school and/or Glasgow's valuable School Welfare Service, they needed a highly personal type of care as regards their leisure. Regular contact with these youngsters *in their homes* would seem to be the first requirement.

From what was seen of the girls in the study there was some case for arguing that they were more 'at risk' than the boys as regards their leisure. In the first place they had less formal education. Fewer of them were still in full-time education, a much lower proportion had stayed on at school as late as 16 or over, a slightly higher proportion had left at the minimum age, and far more were currently in an evening class or getting day release. Girls' shortage of formal education suggests that they ought to be making more use than the boys of formal groups but, in fact, the boys and the girls of the sample contained about equal numbers of non-joiners. The second indication of possible risk related to the girls' jobs. They changed their jobs more often than did the boys and fewer were in an apprenticeship. Their work sounded duller than that of the boys; relatively few talked about its prospects with the enthusiasm that was fairly common among the boys and especially those who were apprenticed. The girls also had a lower evaluation of themselves as workers. Several of the girl Leavers who had been at work for a couple of years were disheartened about the little they had learnt and disillusioned about work in general. It was noticed that just a little extra responsibility or just a bit of training brightened the girl's attitude. The case for much more technical training (and for examining whether substantial increase will ever be reached on the present voluntary basis) of course rests on more than the benefits at adolescence. The level of the girl's job before she marries will affect that of her job (and the quality of her life) in the many years of post-marital employment that lie ahead of today's girl. The above arguments for more technical training are obviously strengthened by the economic one, viz. that it is a shocking waste of manpower to underrate the abilities of girls at a time when the shortage of skilled labour is absolute. As far as industry is concerned the root of the matter still appears to be prejudice.[15]

Early marriage and its concomitant, early courting, were

[15] *A Career for Women in Industry*. Brock. Oliver and Boyd, 1964; *Women, Work and Age*. Le Gros Clark. Nuffield Foundation, 1962.

other risks which were more apparent in the girl's life than the boy's. The fact that menstruation, with its disturbing influences, now begins earlier, adds to the strains faced by girls. So does earlier marriage. In the 9 years 1954-63 the Scottish figure for marriage in which one or both of the parties was under 18 more than doubled, from 1,302 to 2,938. Of the girls in the study, 1 in 3 could be expected to marry before her 21st birthday. That the girls themselves were aware of some of the above matters is suggested in the following little comment from a 16-year-old. She referred to 'parents who do not realise that a girl of fifteen nowadays faces worries about boy friends and money which her mother never thought about until she was nineteen'. An over-early acquaintance with the pangs of unrequited love also seemed to tell more heavily on the girls than the boys. Courting certainly had more influence on the way in which the girl used her leisure. It was mostly she who gave up her interests to follow those of her boy. The dozen or so girls in the sample who were already mothers and/or married were not studied in detail but should, perhaps, be included in the girls 'at risk'. Presumably they had been early courters themselves and, compared with the fancy-free, had probably felt less than the usual need for clubs and classes. By implication they had received that much less of the informal education which membership of a social group provides. As regards risk, the national (Scottish) figures show that it is the very young marriages—the teenage ones—which most often break down. These marriages generally survive the first 3 or 4 years and then the troubles begin. And they go on. Such marriages do not go through an early difficult patch and then settle down, but year after year among the 20 and 30-year-olds those who married in their teens have high divorce rates.[16]

What might counter some of these risks? There are many arguments for getting girls, especially those already in work by 15, to take more part in physical activities. Girls tend to have more sedentary jobs than boys, are more often working on a machine and have no parallel outdoor activity to the boys' scratch football. They also probably have more need than their brothers of the world of play where the rules of adult life are temporarily relaxed and the cares of growing up, especially

[16] Information kindly supplied by Mrs Barbara Watson, a Counsellor of the Edinburgh Marriage Guidance Council.

those associated with ever earlier courting, are temporarily set aside. Girls would probably also respond to more opportunities for practising skills—the Arts in particular—which develop the imagination. The Youth Service, still geared primarily to boys' interests, concentrates much more on physical activities than on music, drama and the visual arts. Opportunities to get around more would also be particularly valuable to girls. Travel, including the relatively local trip, is a great stimulant to the imagination. As regards the ex-junior secondary school girl it is particularly true that it is people—persons—who are the most likely agents to interest the girl in raising the quality of her free time. There was some evidence that the age at which this could best be tackled was in the girl's mid-teens rather than at 15 or so when she was engrossed in a multitude of new experiences. The fact that at about 17 some of the girl Leavers were reading more and that they stayed in more than they had done at an earlier age also suggested some change in their outlook. The glamour of going out to work had worn thin and as any vocational training had probably finished, the girl had more free time. If her job was a poor one this tended to be the age at which she began to realise its limitations. It was also noticed that round about this age certain of the girls appeared to be making up their minds as to whether they should opt for marriage and its inevitable restrictions fairly soon, or try to see something of the world before they settled down. It would have been helpful if Youth Service workers could have talked over such matters with the girl's parents and put the case to them for helping their daughter to develop her whole personality as well as for getting her happily married.

The subject of this study was the 'average', that is the law-abiding adolescent. Indeed its terms of reference required that it should avoid concentrating on the actively anti-social minority. But Trouble connected with adolescents loomed so large in the public eye throughout the study, and impinged so frequently on their leisure, that it could not be disregarded. Moreover, the boys and girls themselves referred to Trouble so often that it was plainly something which weighed on their own minds. They associated it with gangs, large amorphous groups which operated through a few key older boys and many hangers-on to be called up as required. Fighting and hooliganism were the two aspects of Trouble most often referred to.

They did not often talk about stealing, though housebreaking, theft, etc. is the type of Trouble in which the greatest increase has taken place.[17] Most of their fighting was a group affair. Though it frequently took the traditional form of one district marauding another (the Maryhill 'Fleet' were at loggerheads with the Drumchapel 'Bucks') much of it was between the youngsters of one locality. The fights did not seem to be related to definite quarrels or ancient grudges—any excuse would do. Trouble might flare up for the most trivial of reasons, an imagined insult or a bit of jealousy at a dance. The favoured weapon was a knife. They regarded it as only common sense to carry some form of self-protection and to go about in groups. They said that anyone was liable to be set on. A genuine fear of physical assault does appear to be a more common feature in all age groups among working-class society than it is in middle-class circles. Girls were sometimes involved in fights but more often in private than group quarrels. One was heard of who, in a fight with another girl, had her eye put out with a steel comb.

Of those involved in serious Trouble, a small but key minority appeared to be boys in their late teens who had a long-standing reputation for being always mixed up in brawls. They were classed by the other youngsters as an unintelligent lot. And they were cold-blooded, 'He'd knife his grandmother for a bottle of Vordo.' These instigators of serious Trouble were feared as unlike ordinary people. Certain of the youngsters of the study who had grown up in homes near to those of these real Troublemakers recalled them as children who had never been given the small pleasures—birthday treats, outings, nice food—that meant so much at that age.

Another set of those involved in Trouble, and a much larger one numerically, were the boys who looked on it as a pleasurable break in an otherwise tame existence. There was an exciting element of unpredictability about Trouble. 'Once a fight starts *anything* can happen.' This attitude to fighting, combined with the opportunities afforded to prove one's guts, suggested that it was not so far removed from play in the original sense of the word. Of course things often got out of hand but, compared with the key individuals and the violent

[17] *The State of Crime in Scotland.* Shields and Duncan. Tavistock Publications, 1964.

sub-culture of their world, the problems posed by these other boys might almost be described as benign.

It was quite beyond the competence of those connected with this study to comment on the deeper reasons for the prevalence of so much Trouble among the adolescent population. Among the more surface causes, their abundant physical energy was probably one factor. Better health and physique, less exhausting jobs and shorter hours mean they have a great deal of steam to let off. At the same time urbanisation, larger units at school and at work and even the fact that the working-class family now lives in smarter surroundings, all impose that much more restriction on behaviour. Rehousing, too, especially on the scale that has taken place in Glasgow since the war, weakens the social codes that any old-established community sets before, and in general manages to enforce on, its younger members. As seen in Drumchapel, Trouble was also associated with another aspect of rehousing, viz. the abnormal structure of the population. Too high a proportion of young people means that they lack the normal opportunities for learning, merely by observation, how adults conduct themselves. Battalions of police brought in for the odd three or four hours cannot set the round-the-clock silent example of how those who are adult normally behave. It is also worth referring to another matter which may have indirect bearing on the upsurge of Trouble. The argument is that today's Scottish adolescent faces a rather special dilemma. While brought up by parents and schools and churches which, by and large, still hold fast to authoritarian attitudes, he, like any other of today's adolescents, is continually being subjected to pressures from mass media which preach a gospel of 'Live by your own codes'.

Assuming the youngsters correct in distinguishing between the two main sets of their contemporaries who get involved in Trouble, then two lines of action are called for. The 'hard men', the seriously disturbed individuals, could probably have been spotted before they were old enough to exert much serious influence and if so they should be given the special services that their disabilities demand. More of the strap at home and at school, and more of the birch in adolescence would seem a futile answer to the load of problems from which these young people suffer. The other main set of Trouble breeders, those who get involved primarily because they want to liven things up a bit, need many more opportunities for excitement in fields that are socially acceptable. Tough, challenging physical activities are an answer for some. Others just might discover the excitement which they crave for in activities associated with the Arts. Anything that strengthens his imagination helps the adolescent to recognise that there are even more exciting and more sophisticated pleasures than those associated with Trouble. The richer the youngster's imagination, too, the more likely he is to put himself in the other fellow's shoes and thus to avoid the senseless kind of Trouble which starts off just for a lark. The older boys were insistent that the seeds of Trouble are sown before adolescence. Parents supported them here in that they were more often concerned about lack of leisure facilities for their younger boys, those of 9-12, than for their teenage children. As regards certain younger children generally, parents spoke up for the hearty type of organisation which teaches clear-cut codes of conduct. They instanced the Salvation Army and the Mormons. From what was seen in certain parts of Dennistoun and in Drumchapel as a whole there is also a crying need for more to be done for quite little children, the small fry who can be seen roaming the streets late into the night. Two final comments on Trouble as seen in this study are first, that reward is a more effective determinant of behaviour than punishment, and second, that it is not only adolescents who find it unaccountably easy to go off the rails.

Before leaving this section on Trouble some reference must be made to action as regards drinking since the youngsters themselves nearly always associated the two. Might it even be sound to increase the facilities for drinking by lowering the legal age at which pubs and off-licenced premises may be used, and by providing more bars at dances? This would at least encourage young people to drink under more leisurely and civilised conditions than on the street or up the close. At the same time enforce the law strictly and impose far severer penalties, including withdrawal or suspension of licence for the publican who knowingly serves those under age or allows disorderly conduct on his premises. The police could help licencees and bar managers by more frequent visits, with the accent on friendly assistance rather than, as in the prevailing system, by calling only at closing time to check after-hours drinking. One of the team members, a young man who was very familiar with

Glasgow pub life, drew some interesting comparisons between it and the drinking patterns of down town adolescents in New York and in Philadelphia. There he saw less evidence of drinking, fewer cases of drunkenness, and a law which was more strictly enforced. Anyone under 18 in New York city and under 21 in most of the other States had to produce his identity card before he was allowed in licensed premises and the bar manager lost his licence and was fined heavily if caught infringing the law. This observer also noted that the beer was less strong and sold in smaller quantities. Another possible line of attack, especially with the younger adolescents, would be to get them much more knowledgeable about the techniques of drinking. They are going to drink at an earlier age whatever the legal restrictions. Could more be done to show them the ropes perhaps even before they leave school? Young adults would be the ideal people to put them wise to the quality and potency of different wines and spirits and the need for discernment in their use.

The ultimate responsibility for how young people deal with drinking rests, of course, with adult society. It is an open question whether the drink trade should be used for the sake of the national economy and/or for private profit at all. In so far as those still in their teens are concerned, how legitimate is it to subject them to the vast pressures of the trade without at the same time offering them alternatives for their leisure that are equally attractive and adult-seeming? The link between drinking and such aspects of Trouble as violence and promiscuity are not seriously disputed, nor are the disastrous effects (as seen in a few cases by members of the team) on the individual boy or girl. These are facts and they are too serious to be shrugged off with airy references to national traditions, climatic rigours, or 'getting over it while you are young'. Too many casualties take place before the youngster has got over it, quite apart from the unpredictable effects on his later life.

Those who undertook this study were reluctant to make pronouncements as to whether the boys and girls were using their free time in a way that was satisfactory or not. But they agreed on one point, that there was a great deal of 'sameness' about their leisure. To the adult eye it was too often a humdrum affair confined to a routine of pictures, dancing and cafe. It was rare to find a youngster with a passion, or one who seemed to know the happiness that comes from complete absorption. Few appeared to have an inkling of 'all the world's vastidity'. Sheer paucity of imagination was probably part of the problem which is one of the reasons for pleading for the Youth Service to put more emphasis on the Arts. But all three areas were also short of facilities sufficiently cheap and local to meet the youngsters' limited time and money, sufficiently varied to tempt them into new experiences, and sufficiently alive to the importance of meeting social needs as well as providing activities. At the same time it is only fair to say that many of the boys and girls did not seem to be consciously frustrated about their leisure. 'Vaguely dissatisfied' would be nearer the mark. They themselves certainly did not give the impression of being an anonymous bunch of 'just teenagers'. A healthy variety within the species was self evident. This strengthened the belief that a considerable proportion were on the brink of using their leisure in more varied ways, equating all this loosely with a more fruitful use of their spare time. In many cases it looked as if just a little push would probably have done the trick. In saying this it is always necessary to bear in mind that it is a measure of the youngster's education and sophistication to go after things for himself. A considerable proportion, especially among the less able, will take no action until someone —a person—makes it his business to give the necessary encouragement. As regards this push and the Youth Service, many of the boys and girls were oddly ignorant, not of what units functioned locally, but as to just what they did. The Service should make more use of up-to-date advertising methods. However persuasive the advertising or energetic the push, plenty of youngsters will remain untouched, because with them the dimness of their leisure is one aspect of a generally deprived life.

One obvious source for the little push is the educational world. Improvement in the quality and extent of education would almost certainly step up the use made of the Youth Service despite the reluctance of certain youngsters to associate their leisure with anything that smacks of school. But in strengthening the link due respect must be paid to the view that one has a right to find pleasure in one's leisure—'They only live who life enjoy.' It will be no service to adolescents, especially in view of the mounting pressures (to pass that exam, to get on at work, to acquire a boy friend) if the opportunities that leisure affords for relaxation and play get edged out by education. The youngster's work situation is a second place for operating the little push, and here the new Industrial Training Acts are probably relevant. In France, to take an example from abroad, much of the provision for young people's leisure is associated with industry. The contacts made during this study with young Czechoslovak workers also showed how much importance their country attaches to providing good facilities.[18] Could the trade unions take more definite action as regards leisure and their younger workers, and could employers concentrate more on provision, for example a sports ground that serves a neighbourhood rather than confining it to the employees of a single firm? As regards leisure in relation to the youngster's job, those of this study who perhaps had most need of help were the girls in low-level work. A third potential base for the little push is home. The amount of their time which the boys and girls spent at home doing nothing in particular came out strongly. Imaginative experiments need to be made as regards home-based hobbies, however embryonic. More effort could be made to enlist the support of parents. Now that the age gap between child and parent is diminishing there is more likelihood of shared interests. Very many of the parents met clamoured for more facilities for their youngsters. They saw these chiefly as an insurance against Trouble (which it may well be) but at the same time there is also every case for familiarising parents with the idea that today's increase in leisure is not just a chance for a longer lie in bed or for more hours to be filled in any old how, but a matter of vital importance for their child because it means increased opportunities.

No other age group is so continually discussed in terms of morality as that of the adolescent. The boys and girls were certainly not indifferent to all this assessment, most of which is adverse. It seemed to outweigh the fantastic acclaim given to the tiny majority of their generation who achieve fame. They considered that both sides of the popular image of their age group were distorted. Moreover, as they pointed out continually, all this publicity forced them to conform to the label which was pinned on. The adults connected with this study

[18] *Youth in Europe.* Kerr Bowes, 1964.

had no wish to whitewash the youngsters but at the same time they thought much of the adverse criticism unjustified. They also considered that adolescents had certain things to teach the older generation. For example, a lack of preoccupation with status and with money was one of the characteristics of the boys and girls. The importance these youngsters attached to sincerity was another quality much in evidence. It was shown in the 'I HATE PRENTICE' with which one forthright young man ended his (written) comments. Nor was self-criticism uncommon. 'I like pulling objects apart but seldom put them back again', wrote one girl who later said she was 'ashamed of the way I sometimes make fun of people'. The youngsters were also far less condemnatory of adults than the latter of them. Indeed they often seemed genuinely sorry for older people; they got stuck in a rut, did not realise the value of new ways of doing things, and had no idea of how to enjoy themselves. These boys and girls also had something to teach the anxiety-ridden adult world about being grateful for what life offers here and now and letting the morrow take thought for itself. Of all the words to apply to the adolescents of today, 'innocence' may seem a peculiarly inappropriate one. But in an odd way some such quality did cling to them. The writer was also continually struck by the absence of the meretricious in these Scottish boys and girls. All told, and dismissing the question of Trouble which after all only involves a minority, it is hard to understand why society has developed so much coldness towards this age group especially when a sympathetic understanding of younger children is so marked. Is the hostility perhaps related to the new powers which, through no fault of their own, are now wielded by the adolescent? The boys and girls did not mince matters—'They're jealous of us.'

In that any mass labelling reinforces stereotypes and diminishes the individual there is a real need to cut down on some of the strictures. A little more in the way of kindly concern and practical help with their leisure is what would really have helped the adolescents in Dennistoun, Drumchapel and Armadale. There is also a need to recognise that, for all the ballyhoo about Youth, adolescence is probably not a particularly happy stage. Apart from anything else the youngster has to come to terms with the fact that he is not going to receive as much obvious affection as when he was a child. A minority of those met with also had troubles of a more obvious kind. They were only too plainly battling an unaided way as regards their health, their job, the company they kept, and their free time. What these boys and girls wrote down about their life often gave more clues than the interviews on the problems they faced and, vital as regards their leisure, the things they valued.

Fig. 15. Band class, Dennistoun

'What makes you happy?', for example, got this reply from four of the younger boys and girls.

The things that make me happy are when Im away fishing and when the fish are biting. My tropical fish also make me happy when they have young or eggs so I can sell them and make some money.

When she comes and stays with me, and my mother and father are out. She usually stays with me and sleeps with me. I have a double bed so we sleep together. She wears nightdress which you can see through and her chest sticks out. After a time it get warm and she takes it off and we get on with it.

A lot of things make me happy. I like when I am out with a girl I like her to take interest in what I do and say to her. I like to take her places which are not too expensive although it always works out that I spend about 15 to 20 shillings every saterday night. Another thing I like which makes me happy is money and cigarettes although if I am caught smoking I'd get a hammering. I count a good, happy day, a day when my father takes me out and I like taking a fly wee smoke.

Another youngster, speaking up for herself and her friends, wrote that 'Most people condemn teenagers but for us it seems to be a time for living and these years are so short soon the excitement will lessen'.

Many of the questions raised in this study have remained unanswered. One not in dispute is that the number of boys and girls in the 15-19 age group will rise considerably between 1969 and 1979. Currently (1966) Scotland has 431,000 such youngsters. When the school leaving age is raised in 1970 a further 52,000 will be added to those in full-time education, a highly relevant issue as far as the leisure-time needs of the adolescent are concerned. Another likely change is that the amount of free time young people have at their command will increase and, more important, that their leisure will occur at times other than the traditional ones. The climate of opinion on the use to which leisure should be put is also being revised. Leisure's age-old association with the necessity for rest after physical toil is giving way to the conception of leisure as something which affords the chance of a richer life. Though leisure and culture have always been associated they have been regarded as a luxury for the few rather than a need of the many. Today bread and circuses are not enough. There is a heavy responsibility on society to 'awaken, tend and protect' the creative powers of adolescents—those at the age when one really begins to make one's own choices. As Dickens said, reviewing his life before 21, this is the stage 'when four years are equal to four times four'. From what was seen time and again in this study the main drive should be directed towards those who are least able to vocalise their leisure-time needs. By and large this is the young worker whose education has been at a junior secondary school. The legislation relevant to this drive for more extensive facilities is to hand. It is urgent that the implementation should be at a speed which is rapid and imaginative enough to meet the demands made by the rising numbers and the higher standards of today's adolescents. The chief agent in all this is, of course, the Local Authority, but Authorities are relatively powerless unless society recognises the significance of the new freedoms afforded by the increase in leisure. Too many youngsters are still shut off through no fault of their own from what one of them so rightly, at this age, called 'the lovely enjoyable world'.

APPENDICES

Appendix A

NATURE AND VALIDITY OF MATERIAL DERIVED THROUGH INTERVIEWS WITH THOSE AGED 15-19 AT APRIL 23, 1964, AND LIVING AT A SAMPLE OF ADDRESSES IN THREE AREAS

Nature of sample

The problems which hamper drawing a sample of the 15-19 age group were referred to in 'Methods'. Preliminary advice was sought from two statisticians on the staff of the University and from an expert on sampling techniques at the London School of Economics. A simple random sample was unobtainable as no complete list of this age group in each of the areas was available. An estimate of the 15-19 population was based on 12-16 age group at the 1961 Census, and from this was calculated an estimated number of adolescents per address. Unfortunately the address lists could not be used as the basis for a simple random sample of teenagers because it is common in Scotland to find 6, 8 or more households at the same address. A method of taking a random sample of households was discussed but discarded on the grounds of complexity. It must be stressed that the team of interviewers consisted of volunteers and it was thought essential to ensure straightforward instructions. It was decided, therefore, to select a random sample of addresses, and to instruct interviewers to locate all teenagers in the 15-19 age group at all of the households at each address. It was appreciated that it would therefore not be possible to calculate sampling errors with any certainty but (*a*) the need to maintain workable instructions for interviewers was considered to be of considerable importance and (*b*) it was thought that the clustering of interviews was not likely to have a significant effect on the enquiry as a whole.

Though this sampling method had certain statistical disadvantages, it was relatively simple to draw up, which lessened the possibility of error, and it was free from bias. A sample confined to three small areas obviously does not permit the material to be used for generalisation on 'Scottish youth'. On

the other hand, each of the areas has numerous counterparts—
what holds for Drumchapel, for example, is likely to hold for
other of Glasgow's large housing estates.

Validity of material

The discrepancy between the number (633) of adolescents
located in the autumn of 1964 and the number (864) expected
from calculations based on the Census of 1961 is referred to in
'Methods'. The discrepancy was highest in Drumchapel where
only 284 instead of the expected 416 boys and girls were
located. Much thought was given as to how this discrepancy
might have arisen. Errors in drawing the sample were dismissed as unlikely. Two other possibilities were population
movement during the four-year time lag since the Census, and
carelessness on the part of interviewers in administering the
sample. Both points were re-examined and certain checks
devised. Some loss in a 15-19 age group is to be expected since
at this age the older adolescents are beginning to leave home
for work, marriage, the forces, etc. Two of the three survey
areas were undergoing considerable population changes of a
general character. In Drumchapel, movement of population
away from this still unsettled housing estate was said to be
considerable, especially among families whose children were of
an age to be earning and starting to leave home. An analysis
of the City Housing Department's figures, for a 2½-month
period, showed that the last 50 families to move away had a
much higher proportion of children over 15 than had the last
50 who had moved into the area. In the 15-19 age group, for
example, 32 had moved out and only 5 come in.[1] Another
possible source of discrepancy was that the 43 volunteer interviewers had not taken sufficient care in locating every single
adolescent of the required age living at the addresses with
which they were provided. Certain interviewers' lists had
produced a higer proportion of adolescents than had others,
which looked suspicious though it was not necessarily so since

[1] Family composition of last 50 families leaving Drumchapel (as shown
on City Factor's records for Jan., Feb. and part of March 1965). Total =
100 adults, 92 children. Age groups: 0-4(7); 5-9(12); 10-14(26); 15-19(32);
20-24(11); 25-29(4).
 Family composition of last 50 families moving into Drumchapel (March
to beginning of April 1965). Total = 100 adults, 134 children. Age groups:
0-4(78); 5-9(33); 10-14(14); 15-19(5); 20-24(4).

Method of drawing sample and of allocating addresses to be called at by interviewers

Area	Location	Housing	Number of addresses within area (based on Electoral Register)	Estimated pop. aged 15–19 at addresses in area (based on pop. aged 12–16 at 1961 Census)	Adolescents required for interview	Addresses required to produce no. of adolescents needed*	Number of addresses allocated to each interviewer
Drumchapel (Glasgow)	6 miles north-west of city centre (municipal ward minus 1 outlying enumeration district)	Entirely post-war council houses. Multi-occupied tenements	1,582	5,832	400 (approx. 1 in 14½)	113 addresses (to produce 416 adolescents)	6 addresses each to 13 interviewers; 7 addresses each to 5 interviewers
Dennistoun (Glasgow)	1½ miles east of city centre (municipal ward minus 4 outlying enumeration districts)	Mainly pre-1914 privately owned houses. Some inter-war council houses. Multi-occupied tenements	1,179	1,327	200 (approx. 1 in 6½)	197 addresses (to produce 222 adolescents)	20 addresses each to 11 interviewers; 19 addresses each to 3 interviewers
Armadale (West Lothian)	21 miles east of Glasgow and west of Edinburgh (whole burgh plus 4 adjoining enumeration districts)	Mainly inter and post-war council houses. Some 19th cent. houses. Single-household houses	2,517	753	200 (approx. 1 in 3¾)	755 addresses (to produce 226 adolescents)	69 addresses each to 7 interviewers; 68 addresses each to 4 interviewers

* Minor adjustments were made to the figures so as to produce an undistorted workable pattern.

the tenements varied in size. Checks were made on this point. The five professional interviewers, when working on the 79 'cases', checked the accuracy of the record made by the original interviewers at each of these 79 addresses. Error was minimal in Armadale and Drumchapel, considerable in Dennistoun; but it was found that most of the Dennistoun adolescents not originally located had moved into their house since the initial locating was undertaken. In any case the main anxiety about discrepancy was in Drumchapel, not in Dennistoun. A further small check was made of the lists of a few selected interviewers by going back to the families on the original lists and confirming or otherwise the presence of any adolescent of the required age. In this case most of the lists were found to be accurate though just a few contained substantial error. A mistake of course always implied a *loss* in the total figures since the interviewer might have missed an adolescent but would hardly have invented one! The conclusion reached was that the discrepancy in the figures for the total sample was primarily due to movement of population, but no method could be found of establishing, still less of estimating, its extent. Anxiety about the discrepancy was to some extent offset by the fact that the refusal rate was gratifyingly low. As regards the nature of the interviews, these were unhurried and informal which allowed for more material to come out than is possible in the rapid 'yes-no' of many types of interview. When the schedules came to be milled over later on, the additional notes made by the interviewer did much to amplify and interpret the formal answers.

Form Y.W.2

APPENDIX B

GLASGOW EDUCATION AUTHORITY

I. RECREATION AND INFORMAL EDUCATION CENTRES. 1964–5

(A) *Membership and staff of centres and clubs under the management of the Authority, i.e. those Centres the Education Authority has been instrumental in bringing into being and which they control.*

	Number of clubs or units (a)	Approximate number of members (b)	Age Group (c)	Number of general leaders Full-time paid (d)	Part-time paid (e)	Unpaid (f)	Number of E.A. specialist instructors Full-time paid (g)	Part-time paid (h)	Unpaid (i)
1 Play Centres	5	483	8–10		3			20	
2 Junior Clubs/Classes	60+14	7,303	11–13		36			345	
3 Youth Centres*	2	618	8–18		2			25	
4 Youth Clubs	57	12,773	14–18		28			775	

* i.e. Premises used exclusively or primarily as Youth Centres.

(B) *Buildings owned or controlled by Education Authority and used by Education Authority and/or voluntary clubs and centres.*

		Number of premises used exclusively or primarily (a)	Number of premises (other than schools) used part-time (b)	Number of schools used part-time (c)
1	Community Centres	7	—	—
2	Youth Centres	2	1	3
3	Other Centres for informal further education, including training centres, meeting places for independent groups, etc.	—	—	365

II. ASSISTANCE GIVEN BY AUTHORITY DURING THE FINANCIAL YEAR 1964–5 TO
(A) *Voluntary organisations engaged in youth work*

		Number of units or groups	Cost to Authority in the financial year 1964–5
1	Accommodation provided in schools or other premises belonging to Authority	2347	£30,922 0s 0d
2	Grants towards rent and maintenance of other premises	45	£15,615 10s 0d
3	Assistance in cash or kind towards provision of equipment	36	£2,212 0s 0d
4	Grants towards leaders and instructors employed by the voluntary organisations	26	£6,005 0s 0d
5	Supply of leaders and instructors employed by the Authority	234	£20,771 0s 0d
6	Other forms of assistance	26	£2,484 0s 0d
7	Total number of units assisted (units assisted under more than one heading to be counted once only)	2,469	

155

Appendix C

TABLE 3*

Number of people living in home in relation to educational situation of adolescent (%)

	In full-time education	Left full-time education	% of total interviewed
2–3 persons	23	22	22
4–5 persons	55	42	45
6–9 persons	20	32	30
10 or more	2	4	4

TABLE 4

Nature of father's job in relation to educational situation of adolescent (%)

	In full-time education	Left full-time education	% of total interviewed
A Unemployed, invalid, etc.	3	5	5
I Professional	16	4	6
II Supervisory	13	9	9
III Clerical	16	7	8
IV Skilled manual	35	33	34
V Highly paid unskilled manual	6	8	8
VI Semi-skilled manual	2	12	10
VII Unskilled	3	10	9
Father dead	7	12	11

Nature of father's job in relation to full-time education of adolescent (summary)

Fathers (of all adolescents in sample) employed in job type I, II, III	28
Adolescents (with fathers in job type I, II, III) in full-time education	49
Adolescents (with fathers in job type IV) in full-time education	19
Adolescents (with fathers in job type V, VI, VII) in full-time education	17

* Tables 1 and 2 see p. 47, 48.

TABLE 5

Nature of mother's work situation in relation to area (%)

	Mother works full-time	Mother works part-time	Mother does not work	N.I.
Drumchapel	18	30	49	3
Dennistoun	23	25	48	4
Armadale	20	11	63	6

TABLE 6

Type of school or college being attended (by those who are still in full-time education) (%)
Type of school or college last attended (by those who have left full-time education) (%)

	In full-time education M	In full-time education F	% of total interviewed	Left full-time education M	Left full-time education F	% of total interviewed
Junior secondary school	3	4	4	43	41	42
Senior secondary school	61	60	61	25	19	22
Comprehensive school	15	8	12	31	39	35
Special school	—	4	2	—	1	1
Other (e.g. technical college, university)	21	23	22	1	1	1

TABLE 7

Age at leaving full-time education (%)

	M	F	% of total interviewed
15 years	90	94	92
16 years or over	10	6	8

TABLE 8

Attendance (current and previous) at further education class or training school (%)

	Attending currently M	Attending currently F	% of total interviewed	Attended previously M	Attended previously F	% of total interviewed
Evening class	19	10	14	14	18	16
Day release	21	3	11	5	1	3
Other	1	1	1	3	3	3
None	59	86	73	78	78	78

TABLE

Type of current job in relation to type

MALE

	Apprenticeship or learnership to skilled crafts	Employment leading to professional qualifications	Clerical employment	Employment with training lasting at least a year	Other employment	Total
Formal group	36	60	25	40	24	32
Leisure Activities I	62	60	67	40	55	60
Leisure Activities II	92	80	100	100	93	92
None of above	3	—	—	—	1	2

* Tables 9A & B, 10, 11 relate only to those who have left full-time education.

TABLE

Type of current job in

MALE

	Apprenticeship or learnership to skilled crafts	Employment leading to professional qualifications	Clerical employment	Employment with training lasting at least a year	Other employment	Total
Armadale	47	6	6	2	38	30
Dennistoun	50	3	6	2	38	28
Drumchapel	55	4	4	4	33	42

9A*

r types of leisure participated in (%)

FEMALE

Apprenticeship or learnership to skilled crafts	Employment leading to professional qualifications	Clerical employ-ment	Employment with training lasting at least a year	Other employ-ment	Total	% of total interviewed
40	50	48	43	27	35	34
27	25	48	29	44	44	51
80	75	86	100	81	83	87
—	25	4	—	8	6	4

Table 9A & B excludes those unemployed at date of interview.

9B

elation to area (%)

FEMALE

Apprenticeship or learnership to skilled crafts	Employment leading to professional qualifications	Clerical employ-ment	Employment with training lasting at least a year	Other employ-ment	Total	% of total interviewed
5	2	19	3	71	24	27
10	2	45	–	43	24	26
5	2	32	4	59	52	47

159

TABLE 10

Number of jobs held in relation to age (%)

Number of jobs	15	16	17	Age 18	19	Total M	15	16	17	Age 18	19	Total F	% of total interviewed
1	87	61	56	63	49	61	69	65	44	36	41	50	55
2	13	28	34	25	33	28	22	19	38	36	32	29	29
3	—	9	6	3	9	6	3	11	12	21	—	13	10
4	—	2	1	3	5	2	3	2	2	—	—	1	2
5	—	—	—	5	—	1	—	—	5	2	—	2	2
6 or more	—	—	—	—	2	—	—	—	—	—	—	1	1
None	—	—	3	3	2	2	3	5	—	5	—	3	3

TABLE 11

Last week's take-home pay in relation to age and sex (%)

	Age 15–17½	17½–19	Sex M	F	% of total interviewed
Under £3	10	1	9	4	6
£3 to under £5	58	14	36	46	41
£5 to under £7	25	41	30	31	31
£7 to under £9	6	30	14	16	15
£9 to under £12	2	12	8	3	6
£12 or more	—	3	3	—	1

TABLE 12

Last week's spending money in relation to age and sex (%)

	Age 15–17½	17½–19	Sex M	F	% of total interviewed
Nil	1	2	1	1	1
Under 10/-	17	4	9	16	12
10/- to under £1	41	20	27	39	33
£1 to under £3	42	55	54	42	42
£3 to under £5	1	11	7	2	5
£5 to under £7	—	4	2	1	1
£7 or more	—	1	—	—	—

TABLE 13

Smoking costs per week in relation to age and sex (%)

	Age 15–17½	17½–19	Sex M	F	% of total interviewed
Nil	66	51	51	70	61
Under 5/-	7	3	7	4	5
5/- to under 10/-	13	11	11	13	12
10/- to under £1	13	21	21	11	16
£1 to under £2	2	12	10	2	6
£2 or more	—	1	1	—	1

TABLE 14

'How did you spend yesterday evening?' (%)

	Sunday M	Sunday F	Monday M	Monday F	Tuesday M	Tuesday F	Wednesday M	Wednesday F	Thursday M	Thursday F	Friday M	Friday F	Saturday M	Saturday F	Total M	Total F
At home	12	10	6	8	8	10	5	7	3	5	3	3	1	4	38	46
At formal group	1	3	1	1	1	1	2	1	1	—	1	—	—	—	7	6
Leisure Activities I	7	5	6	3	4	3	3	4	1	3	2	2	1	1	24	21
Leisure Activities II	8	4	2	2	3	4	3	3	—	—	3	2	5	3	24	17
Further education	—	—	1	1	1	1	1	1	1	1	1	—	—	—	4	4
No information	—	—	1	—	1	1	—	2	1	1	1	—	—	1	3	6
% of total adolescents interviewed about each evening	27	22	18	16	18	20	15	18	7	10	10	7	7	9	100	100

TABLE 15

'How did you spend the summer (1964) holidays?' (%)

	Age 15	Age 16	Age 17	Age 18	Age 19	N.I.	Total M	Age 15	Age 16	Age 17	Age 18	Age 19	N.I.	Total F	% of total interviewed
Abroad	4	2	4	11	7	—	5	2	4	7	6	8	—	6	5
Away with the family in G.B.	25	15	16	4	15	—	15	22	30	27	21	12	—	23	19
Away	21	32	38	31	48	—	34	16	16	37	42	33	100	29	31
Doing something at home	2	6	8	7	9	—	6	—	5	4	6	5	—	4	5
Just at home	21	31	24	42	17	—	27	41	35	20	23	35	—	31	29
No information	28	15	11	4	4	—	13	20	10	5	2	7	—	8	11

TABLE 16
'*Do you read a daily newspaper?*' (%)

	M	F	% of total interviewed
Yes	88	76	82
No	12	24	18

TABLE 17
'*What kind of magazines do you see regularly?*' (%)

	M	F	% of total interviewed
Pop	18	28	23
Hobby	14	2	8
Women's magazines	2	51	27
Romance	—	18	9
Youth organisation	1	2	2
Sport	7	—	3
General interest	10	6	8
Comics	11	8	9
Story magazines	1	2	2
Other magazines	5	2	3
None	45	19	32

TABLE 18
'*Do you read books?*' (*in relation to current educational situation*) (%)

	In full-time education	Left full-time education	% of total interviewed
Yes	85	42	50
No	15	58	50

TABLE 19

Participation in Leisure Activities I in relation to sex, age and educational situation (%)

	M	F	15–17½	17½–19	In full-time education	Left full-time education	% of total interviewed
Scratch football	39	—	15	20	20	17	19
Snooker and billiards	11	—	6	6	6	5	6
Swimming, golf, other sports	12	9	19	9	11	11	11
Fishing and country sports	5	—	3	2	3	1	2
'On the bike'	4	1	6	1	3	2	2
Walking	13	8	15	9	11	9	10
Good works	2	3	6	2	3	2	3
Visiting	14	32	18	24	21	27	23
Baby-sitting	3	5	3	5	6	2	4
'Out, but nothing in particular'	11	10	10	10	11	8	10
Other activities	6	6	4	6	4	9	6
No Leisure Activities I	37	53	38	47	46	44	45

TABLE 20

Participation in Leisure Activities I during last 7 days (%)

	Scratch football		Snooker & billiards		Swimming, golf, other sports		Fishing and country sports		'On the bike'		Walking		Good works		Visiting		Baby-sitting		'Out, but nothing in particular'		Other activities
	M	F	M	F	M	F	M	F	M	F	M	F	M	F	M	F	M	F	M	F	
	21	—	8	—	6	2	1	—	2	—	11	4	1	2	13	27	1	5	8	6	4 3

TABLE 21

Visit to (a) cafe (b) pub during last 7 days in relation to area (%)

	Cafe		Pub	
	M	F	M	F
Armadale	61	49	10	1
Dennistoun	46	46	12	5
Drumchapel	33	19	13	4

TABLE 22

Participation in Leisure Activities II in relation to sex, age and educational situation (%)

	M	F	15–17½	17½–19	In full-time education	Left full-time education	% of total interviewed
Dancing	62	76	69	69	59	72	69
Cinema	83	81	81	83	80	82	82
Cafe	57	46	51	53	50	52	51
Pub	16	6	3	25	2	13	11
Skating	6	7	7	7	5	7	7
Bowling	3	3	2	4	5	2	3
Spectator sport	8	1	4	6	6	4	5

TABLE 23

Participation in Leisure Activities II during last 7 days (%)

Dancing		Cinema		Cafe		Pub		Skating		Bowling		Spectator sport	
M	F	M	F	M	F	M	F	M	F	M	F	M	F
33	40	49	46	44	33	12	4	3	3	1	—	8	—

TABLE 24

Membership of formal group in relation to sex, age and educational situation (%)

	In full-time education 15–17½	In full-time education 17½–19	Left full-time education 15–17½	Left full-time education 17½–19	Total M	Total F	In full-time education 15–17½	In full-time education 17½–19	Left full-time education 15–17½	Left full-time education 17½–19	Total F	% of total interviewed
Uniformed	15	33	10	8	11		18	11	4	5	6	9
Youth club	19	—	16	9	14		23	11	13	14	15	14
Youth fellowship	12	11	3	1	4		21	11	8	5	9	7
Local Authority Recreation Centre	12	11	1	1	3		3	22	8	11	9	6
Sports club	29	—	7	11	12		18	22	4	2	6	9
Other group	25	33	4	10	11		15	78	6	11	11	11
Additional formal group	4	11	—	—	1		3	—	—	1	1	1
Member of no formal group	39	44	69	65	62		36	11	66	66	61	61
Church service	62	44	34	34	39		64	78	41	43	46	43

TABLE 25

Attendance (by whole sample) at a formal group during last 7 days (%)

	Uniformed M	Uniformed F	Youth club M	Youth club F	Youth fellowship M	Youth fellowship F	Recreational evening class M	Recreational evening class F	Sports club M	Sports club F	Other group M	Other group F	Another group M	Another group F
	9	4	8	9	2	5	1	5	8	3	7	6	1	1